Summoned By Love

S. E. Opra
Holy Apostles Seminary
33 Prospect Hill Rd.
Cromwell, Conn. 06416

By the same author and published by
Orbis Books

Letters from the Desert
The God Who Comes
In Search of the Beyond
Love is for Living

CARLO CARRETTO

Summoned By Love

Translated by
ALAN NEAME

ORBIS BOOKS
Maryknoll, New York 10545
1978

Third Printing, January 1982

The Catholic Foreign Mission Society of America (Maryknoll) recruits and trains people for overseas missionary service. Through Orbis Books Maryknoll aims to foster the international dialogue that is essential to mission. The books published, however, reflect the opinions of their authors and are not meant to represent the official position of the Society.

Originally published as *Padre Mio, Mi Abbandono a Te* by Citta Nuova Editrice, Rome

This translation copyright © 1977 Darton, Longman and Todd Ltd, 89 Lillie Road, London SW6 1UD

U.S. edition, 1978, by Orbis Books, Maryknoll, New York 10545

All biblical quotations are from *The Jerusalem Bible* © 1966 by Darton, Longman and Todd Ltd and Doubleday and Company Inc.

This edition typeset in Great Britain and printed in the United States of America

Library of Congress Cataloging in Publication Data

Carretto, Carlo.
  Summoned by love.

  Translation of Padre mio, mi abbandono a Te.
  1. Christian life—Catholic authors. I. Title.
BX2185.C3513   1978   242   78-962
ISBN 0-88344-470-4

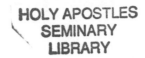
CONTENTS

FOREWORD

I hope people picking this book up will read it calmly and without pre-conceived ideas.

When I wrote *Famiglia Piccola Chiesa,* it caused an uproar in Italy. And that was merely a primer, as anyone can now see.

I don't want the same thing to happen with this one, merely on account of my saying things that we are not used to hearing.

Please bear in mind that what I say in this book is as old as the Bible and, exegetically speaking, is childishly elementary.

It may surprise you that I talk about the Church in a rather unusual way, but I want to make it quite clear that the Church which I am talking about is me, is you, is all of us Christians.

Since the Council, when we talk about the Church, we no longer only mean the Vatican, the bishop and the parish priest, as used to be the case, but the whole People of God.

And the People of God are not likely to take outraged offence at being called self-evidently a nation of sinners, nor at being told that now is the time for them to repent.

The days are gone when, in my own childhood, I had my ears soundly boxed by my mother and was sent to bed without my supper, merely for saying at home that Pius IX would have been wiser not to have excommunicated Cavour (who was trying to unite Italy).

Childish attitudes of that sort should have been banished from devout households by now.

And I want to say something else: let us have no more jeremiads:

- *Our young people are lost to the Church...*
- *Vocations are drying up...*
- *No one goes to church anymore...*
- *It's the end of the world...*

Complaining like this does no good. Indeed, it only serves to spoil the remaining years of our lives, making them sour and spinsterish and poisoning them with impotent dissatisfaction.

Would you like a piece of advice?

Don't keep saying, '*Everything is about to collapse!*' Say, since this is nearer the truth, '*Everything has collapsed already!*' You will find it much more cheering and rewarding to think of yourself as building for a new tomorrow, than as defending a past already old and moth-eaten.

'*Let the dead bury their dead,*' Jesus said. Now, '*Go and proclaim the Kingdom.*'

And, in any case, there is no compelling reason to think that the end of the world has arrived.

We are at the end of an age, and the wonderful thing is that a new age is suddenly beginning, which – in Gospel terms – may well be more fruitful and rewarding.

So try and shed a little of your pessimism.

Try and attend the liturgical assemblies of one or other of the many communities of prayer now springing up like mushrooms throughout the forest of the contemporary Church.

You will find yourself caught up in an explosion of joy and faith rarely to be encountered in the venerable cathedrals of a narrower, more circumscribed age.

And if you do manage to take part in one of these liturgical assemblies devoted to the Word of God and to the Word of God alone, you will certainly come out convinced that the Church is extremely young and is constantly being reborn from the ashes of her past.

For myself, after thirty years of Catholic Action and ten years in the desert, I feel like a child with very much to learn when I am in one of these praying communities.

Take a look, I say to myself, at today's bad lads: they have sent, it seems, everything flying; they have thrown all our pious rhetoric overboard and, with amazing insight and maturity, have replaced it exclusively with the music of the Word of God.

They reply to our old-fashioned devotions by chanting Hosea, Jeremiah, Genesis and Exodus.

And I bow my heart – in humble gratitude.

Fear is a sign of the refusal to be guided by the Spirit

When I think about the state of the world, of the Church which is its conscience, and of myself who am a very small antenna of both world and Church, I feel that we are entering the eye of the cyclone.

A wind is blowing which few of us are used to; and the world, that symbol of stability, now faced with the problems of food-production and progressive pollution, seems unable to cope and unable to feed itself.

The very Church – the City set on a hill, the Mountain of Salvation, the Impregnable Tower, the Unsinkable Vessel – seems, to timorous and under-privileged alike, no longer able to provide the security to which we have been accustomed, and in which those of us with no wish to assume personal responsibility used to find faith and comfort.

Fear lives in the city.

Fear lives in the Church.

That the city should be afraid doesn't surprise me: it is natural that it should, given the rising tide of delinquency and the audacity of terrorists and bandits.

What worries me is the fear inside the Church, for this is a melancholy symptom of the decay of our faith in Christ Risen from the dead, in Christ the Lord of history.

The post-Conciliar Church runs the risk of going down to history as the Church of Fear.

And this is strange, particularly when there is no reason for being afraid! Precisely at the moment when the Church, through the Council, has discovered the miraculous and truly extraordinary assistance of the Spirit (and what institution, whether Christian or not, could boast so new, so clamorous, so free, so fruitful, so innovating, so vital a legislative body as the Catholic Church, in the Second Vatican Council?); when the Church has never had an episcopate more united or more decisive; when it has lived through that unforgettable hour in St Peter's Square at the end of the Council's labours, when Paul VI, his dramatic, kindly features reflecting the hopes of us all – out-going and modern in a way unknown for far too long – offered a new marriage bond between Church and humanity entire; and when it has had the benefit of several harmonious years as the arguments between traditionalists and innovators died away: precisely at this moment, I say, like a plague, this fear-epidemic breaks out.

Take a look and tell me it's not true.

The fear of novelty and the difficulty of seeing things in other terms than in the past, debilitates our dioceses, delays renewal and the implementation of conciliar policies, and often makes those in charge dig in their heels and concentrate solely, if I may say so, on blindly defending old and worn-out forms, instead of becoming tenacious proponents of a Gospel which, in content, is ever new.

And what are we to say about the ones who mistake their own bosoms for the only place where the Holy Spirit can reside?

The fear of disobedience by inferiors makes superiors commit sins of abuse of power, even more harmful to the community of free men, which the Church is.

The fear of empty seminaries and novitiates paralyses the imagination of the Curia and Congregations, exposing their inability to believe that God by no means lacks the strength to provide clergy for himself, nor the imagination to transform them into what he wants. Fear of decreasing church-attendance gives some to think that there is no point in insisting on prayer, since God is no longer to be found inside our cathedrals; the same fear goads others to turn back to the past, when Mass was said in Latin and the very thought of receiving communion in the hand would have caused a scandal.

But where fear has reached its apogee is in the collapse of security: sociologically, politically, culturally, institutionally. The collapse of the historic fabric of a certain type of Christianity – our type – instantly raises doubts about the very existence of God in the breasts of those who, forming part of that Christianity, placed more faith in the visible than in the invisible, and who believed more wholeheartedly in the Christian state and the Sacred Chant than they did in God himself.

And there are plenty of them.

This is no laughing matter.

To have one's faith tested on the cultural level is always one of the harshest ordeals that man can experience.

And when this happens to modern man, already corrupted by power and his scientific knowledge and, furthermore, obliged to live in times such as ours when nothing can be taken for granted any more and past religious attitudes suddenly appear for the childish ones they were, there is no limit to the potential number of deserters.

A man who has hitherto supposed himself to be religious but has never seriously analysed his faith, now reels like a drunkard, having lost both equilibrium and identity.

The heavens are sealed for him, and earth becomes a question mark.

The mental confusion overtaking him can soon cancel out years of fidelity and inner life.

The family falls apart, convents are abandoned, and once flourishing communities come to an end, bereft of strength and light.

And the individual is left alone, without the Church, a prey to his own weakness. And since it is not in his nature to change with the times, the same thing goes on repeating itself, sin having no imagination and thus being eternally and monotonously repetitious.

But perhaps it was inevitable that this should happen.

Too many people deluded themselves that they were Christians when in fact they were pagans.

Too many people separated religion from the Gospel, their church-going from life.

Too many people used to talk about loving the Pope, while displaying no concern about liberating man.

Then again, we may ask without offence: Why does the Church take such a long time to do anything? Why let the Eucharist be celebrated in an unknown tongue for such hundreds of years?

Why nourish people's faith with the pap of devotions rather than with the mighty strength of the Word of God? Why allow the faith of the downtrodden to be ravished away by socialism?

Why such a prolonged alliance with power and wealth?

No need for fear if something is going to change here.

And change in the right direction it will.

What makes me sure of this is that, when the Council asserted the primacy of the Word of God and the faithful began asking questions about the Gospel, the frozen terrain of institutions forthwith began to melt under the action of the heat of the Spirit.

We are undergoing a most extraordinary experience, as though we have returned to the times of Jesus.

The paganism surrounding us and the materialism tempting us are hushed by the song of the Beatitudes, echoing in our souls and filling them with a sense of joy and freedom.

All over the place, small communities of prayer are springing up, identifying with the Church and re-living the Supper of the Lord in gladness and meekness of spirit.

Everywhere, people are talking of freedom for the downtrodden: of service, commitment, poverty, love.

Yes, the Gospel is knocking at the door.

God has not abandoned his people.

The Spirit is still summoning the Bride, the Church.

And the Bride ought not to be afraid.

Fear is a sign of her lack of faith and her lack of trust in Him who is the God of the impossible.

I know it isn't easy, especially for people who are used to feeling secure. For the Church of yester-year, there were all sorts of safeguards.

In many countries, for instance, the Church contrived to have herself cosseted, defended, paid and helped by the state itself.

Church and State: what strength! what power! what support! what a monolithic block!

It seems, however, that those days have gone. And many Christians are glad that they have. Not all, of course: hence, some people are afraid. Very understandably so.

But by living and accepting the Gospel, we learn that it is preferable to rely, not on the power of man, but on the power of Heaven, directly on the Father, as Jesus did. '*My Father and my God.*'

The adventure is more demanding and more rewarding.

The young are all of this party, although they may not yet have quite realised what hardships are entailed in an adventure of this sort.

The adventure of being exiles and pilgrims on earth.

It is the history of Israel all over again.

When I meditate on the Bible, I find that I cannot take a detached view of the pattern of events in sacred history, since my own past and present life seems to conform to the same fundamental pattern. Egypt as the land of slavery, the exodus to freedom, the journey through the wilderness, the entry into the Promised Land, its gradual colonisation, the setting up of the kingdom in Jerusalem, new infidelities to Yahweh, the consequent punishment of the Babylonian exile, the return of the little remnant of Israel and the inauguration of a new age with the coming of Christ.

Wouldn't the Church, which is the New Israel, have to follow the same road?

Wouldn't she have to go through similar stages in her own history?

I think she would.

Perhaps she hasn't yet experienced her exodus and wilderness.

Perhaps she hasn't yet conquered the New Jerusalem: Rome?

Perhaps she hasn't yet faced up to those same sins of excessive trust in herself, of the quest for power, of neglect for the poor, of unwillingness to undertake the hardships of the missionary life.

Perhaps, in perfectly good faith, she has been content to set too high a value on the visible, on the external trappings which in turn have eclipsed the tragic reality of the Crucified, the poverty of the Workman of Nazareth, the frailty of the Infant of Bethlehem.

It may well be.

And it may well be that the time has come for the new exodus – as Hosea says: '*They will have to go back to Egypt!*' (Ho 11:5).

For so much security and splendour, deportation to Babylon seems very appropriate, given that Babylon is what our Christian cities have turned into.

We Christians ought henceforth, I think, to consider ourselves as living in a foreign land, as deportees in a modern Babylon, reduced to tiny minorities but witnessing to the Invisible, no longer as bosses but as guests among the nations, offering a message which has the power to save, offering a hope which is in fact the only hope.

And since we have to begin all over again, this means starting from a much more advanced and complex situation, and all the more explosive for that.

Some people feel pessimistic when thinking about Hosea's words:

'They will have to go back to Egypt,
Assyria will be their king again.
The sword will rage through their cities,
wiping out their children in their midst.'

(Ho 11:5-7)

It may well be that the Church will have hard times, as
Israel had at the time of the Babylonian Captivity – many
harsh, straight-speaking prophecies circulate in the un-
dergrowth of our parishes.

For myself, this doesn't worry me much, since Christ
himself has set me free from fear; hence I am no longer in
Israel's position, to be terrorised by the Assyrian sword.

I feel myself re-assured and comforted by the coming of
Jesus into my life and, as I search the works of Hosea, I
prefer to linger over these other sayings of his:

'Ephraim, how could I part with you,
Israel, how could I give you up?
My whole being shudders at the thought –
for I am God, and not man.'

(Ho 11:8-9)

Behold, I am your God, says the Lord.

And to be God, my God, means that he is my Father,
that he is the root of my existence, that he is Lord of heaven
and earth, that he is the Absolute, that he is the Saviour,
that he is my End and my All.

If God is my God, I need fear nothing.

I put my trust in him.

I let myself go.

He is the God of the impossible.

If a seminary shuts down, it never enters my head to
wonder whether or not there will be a priest to give me Holy
Communion.

If the Vatican were put up for sale, I shouldn't worry or
think that everything had come to an end and that God had
been vanquished by the forces of evil.

Far from it, I should happily sing the same words of hope as Hosea:

'I am the Holy One in your midst,
I shall give a lion-like roar
and your sons will come speeding like doves,
returning like birds to their nest.'

(Ho 11:10-11)

Yes, I am full of hope.

And it is genuine hope, not hope founded on human optimism, but born of my own confusion and weakness, of the Church's confusion and weakness, and of the vision of the eternal Babylon of the world.

My hope is not based on my own strength, nor on the organised resources of the Church, but on the living God alone, on his love for the human race, on his actions throughout history, on his saving will.

I have that hope in God which raised Christ from the dead and which has the power to renew all things.

When I was in the desert, I learnt an extraordinary prayer of Charles de Foucauld's, a prayer summing up my whole faith, a prayer so drastic in content that I could only recite it under the impulsion of the Holy Spirit.

I kept stopping out of dread, unable to go on. Its absolute demands made me tremble, as though they would rob me of part of my personality, would strip me of part of my freedom.

I spent a few years after coming back from the desert the first time, acquiring new experience of what it was like being with people again.

If I were to sum up what I now feel, I could put it very briefly: I have discovered how to be much poorer than I thought I was before.

Now, the more you find of poverty, the more it stimulates you to pray. And when I began using that particular prayer again – which we Little Brothers call the *'Prayer of Abandon-*

ment to God' – I found myself reciting it with greater truthfulness.

Try reciting it yourself, and see if you succeed in getting right to the end in love and peace of spirit.

If you do it will be one more proof that God the Father has sons all over the place, and that the Holy Spirit fills the whole universe with his love.

Here is the prayer:

Father,

I abandon myself into your hands;
do with me what you will.
Whatever you may do, I thank you:
I am ready for all, I accept all.

Let only your will be done in me,
and in all your creatures.
I wish no more than this, O Lord.

Into your hands I commend my soul;
I offer it to you
with all the love of my heart,
for I love you, Lord,
and so need to give myself,
to surrender myself into your hands,
without reserve,
and with boundless confidence,

for you are my Father.

CARLO CARRETTO

Spello, Easter 1975.

PART ONE

God is my father

These simple words proclaim
the most important prophecy
concerning man,
and answer every question
raised by the mystery of life.

Father

First to be made is a star
  next to be made is a son.
First to be made is a flower
  next to be made is a son.
First to be made is a dragonfly
  next to be made is a son.

God made me first like a fragment of star and gave me life, then he designed me like a flower and gave me shape, then he infused awareness into me and made me love.

I believe in the evolution of God's creativity, and I delight in thinking how God takes materials from the rocks to make my body, and designs from the flowers to build up my nerve cells.

But when I think about my awareness, I seek the model in him, in his tri-une life; and he made me in his own image and likeness: communication, freedom, eternal life.

All this amounts to making a son, since the son is life from the very life of the Father, is freedom from the very freedom of the Father, is communication to communicate with the Father.

There are many designs in the visible world and in the invisible heavens, but all are expressions of a single design on God's part: to make a son of me. A son to have the same life as his and to be eternal, the same freedom and to be happy, the same ability to communicate and to be Love like him.

Of course the plan is not yet completed, the work has not yet come to an end. If it had, that would be the end of the world.

The world is still unfinished, there is much work still to be done, and that is why *'the whole creation is eagerly waiting for God to reveal his sons . . . and is groaning in the pangs of childbirth'* (Rm 8:19, 22), since the work is far from easy.

The distance from the end is the distance separating each of us from his true birth, that is to say, from the day when he will emerge from the womb of visible things, to say *'My Father'* in absolute awareness as he turns towards his very Creator to enter his house as a son, not as a picture to go on the wall; as a son, not as a vase of flowers; as a son, not as a beast ignorant and bemused and hence incapable of knowing its father.

The history of man on earth is nothing else but the protracted, dramatic and challenging history of his transformation, that is, the actual gestation of man into son of God.

There wouldn't be anything dramatic about the transformation, if man were not himself obliged to assume one of God's most difficult responsibilities, that is, freedom. Nor would there be a challenge, were it not for the real existence of sin, which is that mysteriously wicked characteristic that makes man capable of saying No to Love and of not accepting God's design.

> *'He came to his own domain and his own people did not accept him.*
>
> *But to all who did accept him, he gave power to become sons of God, to all who believe in the name of him who was born, not out of human stock or urge of the flesh or will of man, but of God himself.'*
>
> (Jn 1:11–13)

Making a son!

God is making me his son, God uses the cosmos and history to make a divine environment for my birth as his son.

He moulds and touches me through created things and little by little makes me aware by the gentleness of his Grace and the strength of his Spirit.

I am inside things, am made of things, but aspire to a life transcending things.

Born into things as son of man, I am becoming a son of God.

Born the first time of my father and mother who gave me the earthly realities, I shall be born a second time as son of the heavenly realities.

Now I am like an immature foetus, midway between my past and future, between the things I know and those I do not know.

It isn't a comfortable situation.

In fact it hurts.

I suffer from incompleteness, from blindness, from yearning.

From incompleteness, because I have not yet been made and I sin by reason of my immaturity; from blindness, because I cannot see clearly since thus enclosed in things; from yearning, because I already have the blood of God in my veins and have patiently to put up with my own sick, turbulent, human blood.

Were I to be told that I had to stay in this situation forever, I should think it very bad news.

That would be like being told, 'You must stay in your mother's womb forever.'

I love my mother's womb, where I was generated, but I emerged from it as soon as I could; I would rather look at my mother from outside, not from inside.

The cosmos and history are like a huge, multiple womb, light and dark, easy and hard, in which my generation is being completed, the *'divine environment'* of my becoming a son.

Yet I have to go beyond this, and so do you, whether you wish to or not.

In my hope, I say, *'Tomorrow will be better than today'*, since

God's logic, God's love, now engaged in making me, point towards the better, not towards the worse, towards life, not towards death, towards communication, not towards isolation, towards happiness, not towards sorrow.

That is why, once I have emerged, I shall look back at the earth which generated me and exclaim, 'At last!'

For a long while earth's womb seemed perfectly comfortable, inhabitable, even fair and joyous, but now I find it constricting.

The nearer I come to the way out, the more compressed I feel and the more I want to pierce the wall of the invisible.

Knowing this, God has hit on an ingenious method, an apt corrective to my wish to escape from and shake off Earth's pressure: *charity towards my brothers.*

Listen to what St Paul has to say about this:

'For life to me is Christ, and death a gain; but then, if living in this body means doing work which is having good results, I do not know what I should choose. I am caught in this dilemma: I want to be gone and be with Christ, which would be very much better, but if staying in this body is a more urgent need for your sakes, I know that I shall go on living and still staying with you.'

(Ph 1:21–25)

It couldn't be better: the inner feeling of someone living by faith and torn between love for God calling him away, and love for the brothers holding him back.

Yes, I would rather go away, but if I can still be of use to the Church, I'll stay.

But when we reach the point when faith becomes so ample and transparent, earth and heaven seem to blend into each other as though they were one same thing.

But not entirely.

And to go away and see the Father's face is always best.

But for the time being, here I am and have to stay. I am here and have to understand why I am here. I should say at once that the word 'understand' which I have just used, is inexact.

Understanding is concerned with my relationship with the things I know, and cannot help me with things which I do not know. How can I understand God, whom I cannot see?

How can I understand his fatherhood, when it transcends me and pre-dates me?

How can a foetus understand its mother? It has to have faith — this is all it can do.

Someone yet unborn cannot ask his begetter to document the wherefore of his existence or lecture him on how being born works.

To let himself be made is the first good quality of every creature —

To stay passive in the hand of the One who pre-dates him, we should say today —

To make himself available, the best and most intelligent attitude for someone who knows nothing of his tomorrow and less than little about the path he will have to tread.

Hence, the right word to have used would be 'to believe' but this is very difficult!

Which of us doesn't wrinkle his forehead at the need to believe?

Yes, believing is difficult.

Difficult, because it is a mature attitude for an immature being.

Difficult, because it is a posture of love and extreme trust for a creature incapable of loving and with unbelief kneaded into his nature.

Difficult, because it is an 'end-result', for a foetus in which all has yet to be resolved.

I am tempted to say — and can assure you that I have given the matter a lot of thought — that faith is really a vicious circle: the more you need it, the less you feel it, the more you want it and the less you know where to find it.

When you don't know where to look next and ought to allow yourself to be led, you then set about seeking a solution within yourself though this in fact cannot come from you; the blinder you become and the more you become involved in leading other blind people.

It is tragic and comic simultaneously. We are like conceited, wilful children looking at the doctor who stands before us, medicine in hand. Instead of reaching trustfully out for it and closing our eyes bright with hope, we curl up like wild animals, letting out prolonged howls and thinking up further follies.

Precisely what man cannot understand, that he wishes to understand.

The temptation is a natural one: like clinging to a known table in an unknown sea lashed by the waves.

Yes, it's natural, but that's not enough.

Faith is a new dimension of life in relation to the invisible.

And it is difficult.

And it would be quite impossible for man, if God, who is Love, had not discovered a solution to the problem.

———————

The solution is the Spirit.

The Holy Spirit, which is the Love of God, is like the wind, '*no one knowing whence it comes nor where it goes,*' turning everything upside down and battering on the doors of Jerusalem at Pentecost.

It is like water soaking into dry ground and making it fertile.

It is like the sun warming and quickening stiffened limbs.

The Holy Spirit, being God's love, God's fertility, God's creativity, comes to visit me and say, '*God is your father*'.

First, the Spirit hints at this very gently, then more strongly, then more strongly still, and so on to the end.

The Spirit is, as it were, his Witness.

The Spirit is a Presence acting forcefully yet gently, which, bringing me the light of truth with '*ineffable groaning*', anticipates my deepest aspirations in the prayer, '*Father*', and so returns to the Father, acting for my helpless self.

Yes, this is the Spirit of Witness present within me, coming and going, coming back and tirelessly returning, for this is Love and Love never grows tired.

In vain you may shout that it isn't true, isn't possible for God to be your Father. The Spirit goes away, lets you swear till you're tired, and then is suddenly back with you again, poised like a dove on the floodtide of your ruins and on the debris of your tiredness, to tell you again, '*God is your Father and you will be his son.*'

It is hard to believe that God is our father, when we look at things from our point of view, but it is even harder 'not to believe', surrounded and dwelt in, as we are, by so pressing a Witness.

Sooner or later, we shall be the ones who have to give way.

And then. . . He is Love and Love is unconquerable, the proof which conquers all proofs.

As Scripture says, '*The proof that you are sons is that God has sent the Spirit of his Son into our hearts – the Spirit who cries, "Abba, Father!"*' (Ga 4:6)

Yes, the Spirit cries and cries.

I feel him so strongly that I can find no more arguments with which to oppose him, and were I to deny him, I should sin against him, I mean, against the Spirit, which would be unforgiveable, as Jesus said (cf. Mk 3:28–29).

And hence, at difficult moments, I prefer to repeat the words in which St Paul expresses this sure truth:

The Spirit himself and our spirit bear united witness that we are sons of God; and if sons, then heirs – heirs of God and co-heirs with Christ.

(Rm 8:16–17)

Father!

This is the essence of the whole revelation, the word summarising the entire Bible, this is the content of the '*good news*', this is the end of all fears.

God is my father in the true, deep, genuine, living sense.

God is my father and looks after me. God is my father and loves me.

God is my father and wants me to be with him forever.

If God is my father, I no longer fear the darkness, since he is living in the darkness too and at the appropriate time will turn the darkness into light (cf. Ps 139).

If God is my father, I can communicate with him, can talk to him, listen to him and say to him, '*My Father and my God*'.

This is truly amazing and the fount of all possible gifts.

With Him I have the gift of life.

With Him I have the gift of truth.

With Him I have the gift of love.

Above all, with him I have the gift of 'home'.

All my experience on earth has conditioned me to the idea of 'home'.

Having a home, being at home.

All the homes which I have occupied hitherto – whether positively or negatively – have only urged, ripened and sometimes embittered the conviction that we are intended to have a home, so as not to be on our own. We are made by relationships with other people. We are made by love, gentleness, self-giving, reciprocity.

We are made to go to a home where we shall have a father and we shall have brothers and where no one will be shut out.

We are made for a home, which should give us a sense of stability, of continuity, of repose.

Yes, we are made for a home where God is father and where all men are brothers.

Salvation-history with its steps proceeding from the

'*Covenant with God*' to '*God living among us*', from the '*Presence of Yahweh*' in the desert encampment to the '*Incarnation of the Word*', is nothing other than the translation into action of a loving plan in which we are all involved, to achieve intimacy with the Absolute God as *Presence*, as *Communion*, as *Unity*.

And when St John in Revelations sees the end of the world in a vision condensing all the messianic truths set in action by the triumph of Christ, 'home' provides the imagery for it.

> *I saw the holy city, the New Jerusalem, coming down from God out of Heaven, as beautiful as a bride adorned for her bridegroom. And I heard a loud voice call from the throne, 'You see this city? Here God lives among men. He will make his home among them; they will be his people and he will be their God, and he will wipe all tears from their eyes, and death will be no more.'*

(Rv 21:2–4)

God will share his home with men and his Presence will be so total in his creatures as to shut out, or rather supersede, the previous 'presences', even that of the Temple.

> '*And I saw that there was no temple in the city, since the Lord God Almighty was himself its Temple*' (Rv 21:22), where the light is no longer earthly light but the very light of God '*and the city did not need the sun or the moon for light, since it was lit by the radiant glory of God and the Lamb was a lighted torch for it.*'

(Rv 21:23)

I abandon myself into your hands

God is my father.

These simple words proclaim the most important prophecy concerning man and answer every question raised by the mystery of life as revealed on this small planet called Earth.

This prophecy hovers over all creation, answers every question, appeases every craving, fulfils every hope, justifies every delay, illuminates the darkness, tells man who he is.

Whoever believes it is in the light; whoever does not believe it stays in darkness.

Whoever puts his hope in it can rejoice; whoever does not hope in it is in anguish.

Whoever loves it has life; whoever does not love it is overshadowed by death.

What meaning can life on earth have, if that life doesn't open into the eternal life of God?

What meaning can human fatherhood have, if man is destined for the void?

Perhaps the logic of life is to end in death?

Perhaps the joy of life closes its curtain on eternal darkness?

Perhaps the fire of Love will be quenched in the embrace of an unremitting frost?

No!

The lowly heart has always known it, and from the prophecy of God's fatherhood, so well expressed by St Paul in his Letter to the Ephesians, '*He has predestined us to be his adopted sons*' (Ep 1:5), has drawn his will to live and the courage to wait.

Under every sky.

In every age.

Yes, man appears on earth already '*called*'. Deep down and little by little he has discovered his vocation as son.

Not for nothing did Tertullian say that man is born '*naturaliter Christianus*', being predisposed and made to hear the message of Christ.

And Christ's message is indeed this '*God is my father – God is your father, O Man!*'

Jesus's whole task was to bear witness with the authority '*of one coming from Above, of one who knows*' to a truth already in action, by proclaiming an absolute already decreed by the Father's love and unveiling a mystery hidden for centuries in God.

But this absolute was already in the human heart.

And this mystery was at the root of it.

I have deciphered it by reasoning from the hopes of the poor and the lowliest.

I have sensed it in the patient and silent way of life of Indians on the banks of the Ganges.

I have seen it in the trusting eyes of desert Arabs, whose *Insh' Allah* (Arabic for 'if it is God's will') testifies to their hope in a tomorrow, uncertain though it be for frail creatures.

Yes, man has intuitively sensed his destiny, however confusedly, and in this has found the courage to live and the strength to wait.

For he deserves to live if God is my father.

For I can wait if God himself is coming to meet me.

———————

Yes, if God is my father, I can be calm and live in peace; I am secure for life, for death, for time and for eternity.

And what security is mine!

It becomes a blasphemy to ask in alarm, 'In the year 2000, there will be seven billion of us on earth: who is going to feed us?' given that God's granaries and imagination are vaster and more capacious than my fear.

If God is my father, I count for something and in him find my own true dignity.

If God is my father, I shall not go on saying *ad nauseam*, 'Why?... Why?... Why?' Instead, I shall be realistic and trustfully say, 'You know... You know... You know.'

If God is my father, I shall not attribute the abundance of the harvest exclusively to fertilisers and the quality of the seed, but shall make a habit of repeating what he himself has suggested that I should say, *'Give us this day our daily bread'*, bravely and peacefully trusting to the vagaries of the seasons and the unfolding of history.

If God is my father, I shall not attribute daily events to chance but shall consider them as signs of his love.

If God is my father, I shall not suddenly cease to believe when confronted by some natural disaster, because I can't for the moment see the link between love and adversity, between God's existence and the pain afflicting me.

God is God and is the Lord of the Universe, even when the earth quakes and the rivers overflow, and he is my father, even if my hands get frost-bite and an accident makes me a cripple for life.

His being God and being Father means for me, his son, that, all things notwithstanding, he can transform what we call evil into good and can order events for good which to us seem mysterious and baffling, as says the word of Scripture, *'God treats us as sons. Was there ever a son whose father did not correct him?'* (Heb 12:7).

But here we come to the real problem confusing our sense of what is real, especially for anyone not yet strong in faith and with a limited vision of the Whole.

Between the prophecy proclaimed by the word of God and what I see with my own eyes, there is a conflict, a sort of permanent objection, yes, even cancellation.

I might therefore think that what I see has been arranged by Someone or something to cancel the prophecy.

Says the prophecy to Abraham, '*Look up at the sky and count the stars if you can. Such will be your descendants*' (Gn 15:5).

To which visible fact replies, '*How is this possible? You are a hundred years old and your wife Sarah's womb is sterile and worn out with age.*'

Says Jesus over the bread and wine, '*This is my body, this is my blood.*'

To which the listener's reason replies, '*How is this possible? This is intolerable language*' (Jn 6:60).

Says Jesus when speaking of himself and of his immediate future, '*In three days time I shall rise again*' (Jn 2:19).

Blurts Thomas when he hears the news that the others have seen the Risen Christ, '*Unless I put my fingers into his wounds, I shall not believe*' (Jn 20:25).

And this is why, when I prophecy '*God is my father*' over the cosmos and over the objections apparent to my eyes, everything replies, 'Delusions! How can this possibly be? Look at the injustices, look at the hungry, look what a hell human life has become! How is it possible that God can be my father? My child has died – how can God possibly be our father?

'A car has run me over and ruined my life. Why didn't he intervene?

'I've worked all my life to buy my own house and live in peace. Now a fire has burnt it down. Why didn't he help me?

'I was happy with my wife and children. I was beginning to make good after endless sacrifices. Now I'm suffering from leukemia, which is slowly destroying me. How dare you tell me that God is my father?'

Yes, it is no easy thing to answer these objections.

It is no easy thing to believe the prophecy springing from the Word of God.

And this is why I shall never cease to say that the most exhausting thing in my life has been believing.

And I think this must also be true for you.

Believing does not belong to the natural order; it is a divine element in us already.

Christ's presence in the Eucharist or his resurrection from the dead cannot be affirmed by reason.

Only by faith.

And faith is a theological virtue placed in us by God as and when he wishes.

I know that the visible reality contradicts the invisible reality, I know that earthly events are incomprehensible and constantly in conflict with the eschatological vision of the Kingdom.

But I also know, and have experienced this a thousand times, that when 'I believe' and affirm with all my strength that the word of God is eternal and that the prophecy will come true, I upset the real, I overcome my own gravitational weight, I enter the orbit of light, I live a divine reality, I realise the Kingdom within me, I conquer the world surrounding and trying to stifle me.

When I believe, I am no longer a mere man, I am already a son of God.

And I am the son of a God who is the Lord of the Universe, who presides over a Kingdom which recruits its citizens on earth but, having recruited them, leads them towards another mysterious reality no longer of here-below.

Indeed, He said emphatically to the man who asked Him if He was a king, '*My Kingdom is not of this world*' (Jn 18:36).

This is a difficult truth to remember. The visible keeps making us forget the invisible. '*This world*' conditions us so thoroughly that we find it hard to think that another exists.

And we are constantly bewildered; worse still, are scandalised.

If a child dies, we question the invisible with a grief-stricken 'Why?'

If, having built a house, reared a family and lived with

sons and daughters, we are left alone in old age to witness the collapse of our past, we are again bewildered. Clinging desperately to the fragments, we lash out to prolong our sojourn here a little more, without realising in the least that the invisible realities have to absorb us, to transform and carry us away from the realities of earth.

The earth is not an end in itself.

What I see now is only a beginning; I shall see the sequel later.

If the earth were an end in itself, it would be unintelligible, positively hostile.

If it were an end in itself, if our painful human story ended here-below, it wouldn't be hard to identify the Person who had thought of it, built it and set it in motion, as a criminal.

You are bewildered by a street accident, in which someone breaks a limb or a pretty girl gets her face disfigured?

Go into a lunatic asylum and see if the whole place isn't one gigantic street accident, in which incomprehensible human deformities are raised to the power of infinity.

You are shocked if a military regime administers a few nights of torture to a guerrilla, caught off his guard in the jungle?

Why, then, not be shocked at the appalling torments inflicted on people, in the natural course of events, by cancer which may take months or even years to kill them?

No; no amount of reasoning can convince me that the earth is an end in itself or that creation is limited to the terrifying lives we have to lead.

No amount of arguing can explain to me why I, through no wish of my own, should find myself in this immense cats-cradle of history being obliged to live out a reality which, as the Psalmist says, is *trouble and anxiety* (Ps 90:10).

Everything round me is so terribly incomplete, incomprehensible, temporary, painful, arbitrary, that, if I did not consider it as part of a whole, a first time introducing other times, a beginning to be explained by subsequent development 'beyond what I see', I couldn't help pressing charges against God for having made things so badly, e.g. an earth so full of holes as to cause earthquakes; skies so insane as to destroy the hovels of poor fisherfolk.

Faced with reality, the whole visible reality as my unaided eye perceives it, I have no other choice: either I curse it as the degenerate daughter of an insane father, or I accept it as a mystery.

The Spirit of God living within me tells me to accept it as a mystery.

And bears continuous witness to this, to me.

And I bear witness to it to my brothers and tell them, '*Yes, God is the Lord of the Universe.*'

And he is Lord even when the sea is tempest-tossed.

He is Lord even when I suffer and mourn.

He is Lord even when my house gets blown away.

He is Lord even when my hour comes to die.

And the hour of death is when I shall have my explanation.

That incomprehensible moment for me as son of man will be the moment of illumination for me as son of God.

Dying, I shall understand the wherefore of life.

Dying – like an atom compressed by the weight of the whole universe and heated by the limitless temperature of love – I shall explode into God's eternity.

Death is the gate to Resurrection.

Death is the entrance to fulness of life.

Death is the greatest secret to be revealed.

Do with me what you will

I think about death.
I try to see it as life, as wood needed for the fire
as a field in which a treasure is hidden
as a book to be opened
as seed which has to flower
as a secret which I have to know
as a crossing which I have to make.
The word applying most accurately to death is really the
last one: '*crossing*'.

This was typified by the Hebrews' crossing of the Red
Sea, and actualised by Christ's 'crossing' through his own
Exodus on the night of the Resurrection.

It is the instant which precedes the light.
It is the state of waiting.
It is faith in God the Creator.
It is hope placed in the God of the Impossible.
It is the love required before you can really possess love.

The one who has explained all this and made it so, is
Jesus.

Jesus the first-born Son.
The first to rise from the dead.

And, having made the victorious crossing, having first
paid the price, turns to us and says, 'Do not be afraid. I
have overcome the world' (Jn 16:33).

What occurred on the night of the Resurrection
henceforth concerns us personally.

It was indeed the 'crossing' of all mankind in Christ,
head of the Body which is the Church, and first of all the
saved.

What occurred is so extraordinary that the Church seems

to be mad with joy when she sings the *Exultet*.

And to see someone rise from the dead is enough to send anyone mad: life rekindling in the extinct ashes of human nature, the sudden blaze exploding from the darkness.

This means that God is God, that life goes on and that there is an explanation for all things, even those most baffling or apparently shocking.

It means that man is eternal and that death, which used to frighten him so much and painfully dominate his existence, is now explained, understood, taken captive and conquered.

Now I can laugh, laugh too about my former fears.

Now that I have seen the Risen Christ, I can face my own death with the certainty –

That I too shall rise again.

But let me try and extend the concept of death as 'crossing' to what happens to us every day, every hour, every second of our spiritual and physical existence.

Generally we apply the word death merely to the moment when we expire, to the one which puts an end to our earthly existence.

But the reality is deeper and more all-embracing; death is not, I think, only something concerned with the last day of our lives, but, as I was saying, with every day of our lives.

Every second of our existence, by its nature, contains a painful element of death and, at the same time, by virtue of Christ's resurrection, a true and explosive element of resurrection.

These two realities are hidden within us, just as Christ's death and resurrection are hidden within us.

'*In our body we always carry the death of Jesus, so that in our body the life of Jesus may always be manifest too.*'

(2 Co 4:10)

The conflict between the two realities is the crossing into

the Kingdom, that Kingdom which Christ has already declared to be *'present within us'* (Lk 17:21) and which is developing and expanding until it reaches its completion at the end of the world.

It is the transition between the visible and the invisible, the frontier between human nature and divine nature, the fruit of every good desire, the value of every sacrifice, the ratification of every loving deed, the genuine slow gestation into sons of the Father.

Yes, the duality 'death-life', to which Christ's own death and resurrection have given seal and explanation, plenitude and the promise of irruption into the Kingdom, is unquestionably the key to all the why's and wherefore's that torment us, and the right answer to the objections raised in the human heart.

Death and life, taken together and particularly when in conflict, signify the beginning of things, the perennial evolution of the creation, life's successive leaps forward, the splendid days of Genesis, God's way of going about begetting his son and passing on his own experience of love to him.

Our dying to earth is a progressive emergence from the womb of matter and history, so that we may gradually acquire the stability of the Kingdom and full communication with God.

If things are as the Gospel of Jesus tells us and as the hope within us maintains, we ought to change our perspectives and get used to seeing things as a reflection of a truer reality.

Earth is an image of heaven, not heaven an image of earth.

The sun is an image of Christ, not the other way round.

Everything I see betokens what I do not see, draws attention to it, underlines its meaning.

Everything betokens an invisible reality far more important than the visible reality.

What is to come is more valuable than what has already come.

Tomorrow is better than today.

What I have betokens what I shall have, which will surpass it, as a child surpasses a foetus, as maturity surpasses immaturity.

Yes, tomorrow is better than today, and this certainty is given me by faith in God, who is Love.

And love goes forward, does not turn backward.

Love creates, does not destroy.

Love lives, does not die.

Opening my eyes to human life, I have to get used to seeing everything as an image of that divine life nourishing me day by day, transmitted to me by Christ.

My father and mother betoken another father and another mother whom I shall have in the Kingdom; the home, once peopled with my children, although today no more, destroyed by the passing years, betokens another home never to be destroyed.

The brothers and sisters who used to live with me betoken those other brothers and sisters who will live with me in the Father's eternal Kingdom.

The food that nourishes me, the fire that warms me, the hills that raise my spirits, betoken another food, another fire and other hills to be mine in the Kingdom.

The liturgical assembly to which I belong, the very Eucharist which I so joyfully receive, are living tokens of another Assembly in which I shall take my seat in the Kingdom, nourished at last by the one food worth receiving: God himself.

How lovely it is to think how everything is an earnest of the invisible world in which I am immersed, as faith lets me discover it piece by piece: hope reviving me and love making it mine!

All is image!

But if from image to image we leap ever higher, we reach the paradise of Him whose image is love or home.

The home where one is loved is paradise.

Elsewhere it is called heaven, elsewhere, kingdom.

But it is the same thing.

And here lies the basic tension affecting man on earth.

When I was in the desert at Tamanrasset or at Beni-Abbes and used to see the hippies – the brave, real hippies, that is – going by on their travels, I was able to assess the seriousness of their wanderings by the number of years which had elapsed since they last saw their homes.

The longer the time had been, the slower they went and the happier they were to stay a long time in fraternity with us.

They had left their own homes which they did not love, their own world which they detested, the structures from which they had fled, and set off in search – often without even knowing or meaning to – of another home, another world, another structure, which would correspond with and express that ideal world, that ideal structure, that ideal home, the blueprint of which lay deep within their hearts.

This is inevitable.

Man on earth seeks a home. . . Home.

And he seeks it as somewhere where he can live, breathe, love and rest.

Those who, like orphans for instance, have never known what it is to have a real home, seek one with painful persistence.

Those who, on the other hand, have had a home, but a bad one, loveless, disturbed, a home where there was strife and hatred, spend their lives seeking the opposite of what they have experienced and in the end are still emotional cripples.

What traumas grip those who have not been loved!

What agonies rack those who have had no home!

The concepts of home and paradise coincide. No one can

rid himself of this unconscious element in his nature, since home, like paradise, is the claim made by the first commandment put into his heart by God.

You seek a home because you seek love.

You seek paradise because you seek love.

Love is paradise, lack of love is hell.

Man has to love, just as he has to breathe, as he has to eat.

'He who loves is in life; he who does not love is in death' (cf. 1 Jn 3:14).

There is no deluding oneself over this, not even when hoisting the banner of justice.

Only love wholly satisfies man.

And hence God puts love at the summit, as it were, identifying himself with his own Love.

Love is man's life, his nourishment, his completion, his ecstasy, his fulfilment.

Without love he cannot live; one glance at the opposite is enough to understand what hell is.

Hell is the lack of love; here on earth we have proof of this already.

And love exerts a constant tension.

All the loves that we discover and experience one by one in the course of our existence: food, friendship, sex, culture, goodness, justice, light – are only partial stages preparing, developing and purifying that total, holy love which is the fulfilment of all loves: love of God, which will be our heritage forever, the devouring fire of our paradise.

Then we shall understand why we were born, why God has summoned us into existence.

This is how the Bible puts it (Dt 6:5 f):

Shema Israel – Shema Israel
Adonai Elohim, Adonai Ahad
Hear, O Israel, hear O Israel,
Yahweh is our God, Yahweh is One.

You are to love Yahweh your God
with all your heart
with all your mind
with all your strength.

Fasten these words of mine
as a sign on your wrists
as a sign between your eyes
on the doorposts of your house and gates.

Teach them to your sons, O Israel,
say them over when you are at home,
when you are out and about,
when you lie down and stand up.

This is the first life-giving commandment
and the second is like it:
love your neighbour as yourself
and you will have eternal life.

———————

Come then, death!
Come, I am waiting.
You do not frighten me any more.
I no longer see you as my foe.
I see you as a sister.
I look you in the face.
I understand you now.
And as you come towards me, I tell you, thinking of him
who holds you firmly in his mighty hand, '*Do with me what*
you will'.
Wholeheartedly I say this to you.
Truthfully I say this to you.
Lovingly I say this to you:
'*Do with me what you will*'.
Accustom me to this extreme abandonment.
Accustom me to this never-ending test.

to this never-adult kiss,
to this never-given change,
to this never-finished conversation.

Accustom me little by little, by distributing my death through all the days of my life.

Put it on my bread like ashes or sand, so that I do '*not live by bread alone*' (cf. Mt 4:4).

Put it in my house as '*something lacking*', so that I do not accept the limitations of the visible.

Put it as insecurity into my security, so that I may only be secure in Him who is the Absolute.

Put it as a reminder in the midst of my joys, so that I may grow used to being alone, as in that second when I shall be alone with you.

When my father was dying, he asked me to stay beside him. He had confidence in me and we were devoted to one another.

God granted me the grace to spend his last night at his bedside.

I sat beside him, holding his hand, and could tell from the way he squeezed mine what he wanted to say to me.

It was as though he wanted to lean on me, though he stared straight ahead.

Little by little, he grew more alone.

As he left the earth for the frontier of the invisible, he was alone.

No one could help him.

He was alone.

Yes, he did in fact die alone.

All help counts for nothing.

We are alone with God.

In the crossing, only God's hand can take you by the hand.

I took my hand away.

Only to God, at this point, can we say, '*Do with me what you will*', for he alone, being God, cannot disappoint our hope.

Whatever you may do, I thank you

What do you want to do with me, Lord?

Your Spirit has told me and keeps repeating within me, '*I want to make you my son*'.

I have summoned you out of nothing to be my son.

I have made use of the whole cosmos to make your body.

I have copied my own divine nature to make your understanding.

I have been summoned by love to live in you.

Now that I live in you, you are to be mine and I am to be yours.

Mine to make you more mine.

Mine to have you with me forever.

Mine to make you like me – free.

Mine to teach you to love as I love.

And why, O God, make me wait so long to see your will accomplished?

Why have you taken geological ages to make me a body?

Why such thousands of years to give me a history?

Why a whole lifetime of immaturity to obtain one glimmer of true light from me – a pinch of love the size of a mustard-seed?

Couldn't you have made me your son immediately?

And a son at that who would know how to love?

Why the time?

Why the waiting?

Why the risks of so long a journey?

Perhaps you will never tell me why, out of all the thousands and thousands of ways available to your wisdom, you chose this particular one to make me your son. Perhaps you want us to discover this for ourselves.

You chose which road should lead from chaos to harmonious unity,

— from Genesis to Apocalypse,

— from conception to birth, from insentience to the marvels of awareness,

— from pre-history to history, from human love to divine charity.

It is the way of living evolution.

It is the way of experience.

It is the way of dialogue.

It is the way of seeking.

It is the way of faith.

It is the way of hope.

It is the way of love.

Whenever I try and think about what you are doing in me, I get a distinct impression that you never want to exert force on me.

No, you proceed by suggestion, suggestion made in silence, in limitless silence, willing to wait until the end of the world.

Your silence is so great and your waiting so deep-seated that the less aware run the risk of mistaking these for death: the death of God.

But this is not so, and I know it.

You suggest, you keep silent, you wait so as not to force us.

You want us to be the ones to come to you; you want us to come of our own free will.

For freedom is what you want to train us for.

The only danger for God, to our way of thinking, is his being omnipotent, and this is a risk you do not wish to run.

So!

You create and hide your creative power so well that you

give all created things the impression that they have made themselves.

You call your people to salvation, you lead them across the desert, you feed them with manna, you quench their thirst with water from the rock, you flatten the walls of Jericho, you conquer the Promised Land for them and, when all is done, your people are convinced that there was no need for you and that what was done was done by their own ability and strength, not by yours.

So convinced indeed that, at the first opportunity, they abandon you and go in search of any old idol to worship.

The reason why is that you are very astute – no one is better at hiding than you are.

Your servant Isaiah loved to describe you as a '*hidden God*' (Is 45:15).

You hide in the creation.

You hide in history.

You hide in the Incarnation.

You hide in the Eucharist.

You hide within us.

You hide all the time.

And you want us to discover you. . . like this. . . on our own. . . in our own time. . . when we need you.

Generally need is what impels us to seek you.

The need for the absolute, for eternity, light, freedom, love.

Above all, we seek you in our difficulties, when we no longer know which way to turn, when we are disillusioned by our pleasures.

But even then you hide what you are doing and give us the impression that we ourselves are conducting the search.

I believe that your motive is always the same: you do not want to force us.

You do not want a marriage of convenience, you do not want to damage our freedom.

And when we get up and come to you, taking the road prepared by you from the outset, we feel perfectly free.

We have no conception whatever that we are putting our feet into the very footprints made by you in approaching us.

How long it takes to grasp that you are existence and will, inspiration and accomplishment, design and history!

I have discovered this in the darkness of faith.

Wrapped in this, I have divined the place where you meet on free terms with man, the divine environment where you 'make him into a son' without conditioning him by your power, without terrifying him with too much light.

'O Yahweh our Lord, how glorious your name throughout the world!'

(Ps 8:1–9)

'And how far above our thoughts, your thoughts!'

(Cf. Is 55:9)

———————

The way chosen by God for making us into sons and hence able to have a loving relationship with him, is the way of evolution, the way of experience, the way of seeking, the way of dialogue, the way of history.

And to be that, it has to be the way of freedom.

Without freedom, there would be no seeking, without freedom there would be no dialogue, without freedom there would be no love.

Everything would be conditioned, orchestrated, cut and dried.

Everything would have the inevitability of a chemical reaction, would be as boring as a display of folk-dancing mounted by a totalitarian government.

But God's taste is altogether different and, having chosen Earth as meeting-place between him and us, has made it the meeting-place

    between chaos and harmony
    between light and darkness
    between life and death

between hate and love
between heaven and earth.

In this contrast-ridden environment, man freely gambles with his own salvation.

Creates his own city.

Carries out his own design.

But in creating the city and carrying out the design, his own hands are hard to distinguish from God's creative hand; man's ploughshare cuts the same earth as is God's earth; his existence as son of man takes the same form as his existence as son of God.

How hard it is to distinguish who does what!

Who can grasp the mystery of this marriage?

Are you at work, O God, or are we?

Is it our work producing the grain, or is it your mysterious will?

How far does your activity extend and where does ours begin?

Some people say, 'All is from God', and others reply, 'All is from man'.

Both are probably saying the same thing.

The design even seems the same; it is not hard to trace.

For the pure and simple-hearted, a mere look at a bird's nest or at a mouse-nest is enough to detect the inspiration behind the entire design.

Who can tell whether the design is God's or ours?

Thus, we look in wonder at a sparrow's nest and would be hard put to it to find a better symbol for the Kingdom which you in the fulness of time have described to us and towards which you have set our course.

Nest, lair, home, love, stability, peace, cooperation, mutual affection, solidarity, universal brotherhood.

What difference can there be between what you suggest to us and what we ourselves feel?

Don't they seem to be the same thing? – And the parables of the Kingdom evoke such a deep response in us because we joyfully recognise them as being true.

They could have been written by any one of us.

But is the original design yours or ours?

Do you make us for you, or do we, athirst for you, invent you?

Was it you who inspired the 'Lord's Prayer' or is this the quintessence of prayer produced by us?

Things tally to such a degree that many people are of the opinion that, had you not existed, we should have invented you.

We can never tell whether the prompting comes to us from you, or whether chance produces it within us.

Whether you wanted to be our father, or whether we ourselves wished to be your sons.

Whether you prompt us to love, or whether we discover that we want to love.

Yes, the God of faith,
the God of the creation,
the God of the Church,
the God of men,
are all the same person.

Our footprints are planted in the footmarks already made by you.

If I had to define you, all I should have to say would be, 'You are he who has anticipated me'.

But where things get more complicated, or rather much clearer, is in the doing.

In comparing the ideal with the reality, we see the gap.

We dream of one thing and we do another.

We want the good, and we do the bad.

We talk of love, and we hate.

Where there is light, we put darkness.

Where there is joy, we sow sorrow.

How disastrous, the building of the earthly city!

A veritable Babylon!

And it always has been!

We cannot deny that we are adepts at going backwards or nearly backwards along the road which we have freely chosen.

Instead of creating a city as free and serene as a nest of larks, we construct a robbers' cave.

Could any sight be sadder than the city of man as exemplified by New York, Tokyo, Hong Kong, Chicago, Belfast?

Someone dying of hunger here, someone of over-eating there.

Someone dying of boredom here, someone of exhaustion there.

How is all this possible?

Why does our history have to be one of selfishness, oppression, violence and sin?

The thought of it is enough to discourage and perplex us, especially when we face the fact that these evils are not situated in the remote past but in our own day when we, enlightened as we suppose ourselves to be, are at work, building the city.

Did ever a period present such a nightmarish picture of war, genocide, torture, concentration camps and death from starvation as ours?

What a stench of corpses pervades our society technically so advanced!

No, no, we have nothing to be proud of when judged by our actual shortcomings.

But surely contemplation of these shortcomings must convey something to us?

If originally we were not able to tell what was ours and what was God's in the design, the evidence from our failure to carry it out can hardly leave us in any doubt now.

Aren't we finally forced to distinguish between what is God's and what is ours?

Yes, from our botching of the design, we rediscover God

as distinct from our own evil-doings, and on account of these can pin-point the contrast between ourselves and his Gospel of salvation.

In the depths of our own sin, we rediscover God; deep in the abyss of evil, we sense him to be near.

In our weakness is when we feel the need for him.

Even if the prodigal son – he is in each of us! – did not know his father properly before leaving home, on his return in such a sorry plight he understood what kind of man he was, since the father's overflowing compassion, then revealed, provided him with all the evidence he needed.

I believe that God never reveals himself better to man than in the abyss of human wretchedness.

Wasn't it in Babylon that Israel rediscovered God, and in that fearful loneliness and gloom that the true hope was born?

The hope that was to sustain the little 'remnant' and prepare it to welcome the distant messianic age?

And the messianic age awaits us too, is ever at the gate, since we are no different from Israel.

Indeed, we must think of ourselves as each being Israel.

And just as in its weakness Israel discovered the true mystery of God, so we shall rediscover God in that same way.

That is the path we have to take if we are to make the earthly city conform as nearly as maybe to the design of the heavenly city lodged within us; revealing us to ourselves as we really are, serving as proof of our maturity or immaturity, spurring us on to doing better and better, keeping our ideal before our eyes and, above all, stimulating our thirst to find – beyond the mystery of human nature – that source of life divine which alone can achieve the impossible on earth: I mean a loving life led by free men.

Is this utopian?
Of course it is.

Everything that God prompts man to be or do is on such a scale as to be classed utopian.

'You must be perfect, just as your heavenly Father is perfect'.

(Mt 5:48)

Utopia!

'Love one another as I have loved you.'

(Jn 13:34)

Utopia!

'Do not judge.'

(Lk 6:37)

Utopia!

'Bless those who curse you.'

(Lk 6:28)

Utopia!
This is the Utopia of Love.

And by seeking to live this utopia which we can never ourselves achieve, we come to know the two great unknowns: God and Man.

And to set them face to face.

And in accordance with God's eternal design, to make them, one the Father, and the other the Son.

I am ready for all, I accept all

If I had to draw something to symbolise the theme of creation, if I had to provide a key to the mystery of our existence, to the darkness in which we are enveloped and im-
prisoned, I should not hesitate to draw a woman's womb
with a baby gestating inside it.

At the heart of the cosmos, the softness of the womb, the
fact of a creature coming into being, the mystery of a life
fertilised by love and itself reproducing the features of its
begetter, admirably represents what is happening to each of
us being begotten by God.

The entire cosmos is no less than the enormous 'divine
environment' of our birth as sons.

All history is no less than a succession of episodes directly
bearing on that maturing foetus enveloped in time and
space, gradually approaching the door leading out of
matter: 'the breaking of the waters'.

The day of each man's birth coincides with the day
when, no longer enclosed in or made of matter, he leaves for
the beyond for good and enters what Jesus has defined as
the Kingdom.

Now, in time, all is womb, all is gestation, all is environment, all is process, all is transitory in relation to the
Kingdom, which, although already within us, has not yet
reached completion.

And it is dark because it is the womb, and it is painful
because it is gestation, immaturity.

This is the way God makes us, forming us by matter,
making us by events, moulding us by history, as a mother
builds a child with her milk and warms it with her love.

What takes a long time and is difficult to grasp is that in this task there are two people at work, not one.

Just as you have mother and child, so you have God and man.

Although there may often seem only to be one – so united are they – in fact there are two.

Sooner or later, one says to the other, 'You'.

The discovery of the 'You', of the other, is made in faith.

In faith, we experience the divine person begetting us and, although he is still unseen, we begin to call him 'Father'.

But this takes a long time.

Some of us go on looking and thinking for years and years, without saying anything.

Then, unexpectedly, we don't know why, in the stillness of the night, or in a white sunlit street, we begin to say, 'Father'.

And we smile.

That is it.

Succeeding in saying 'Father' sincerely and lovingly means that an important stage in divine regeneration has been reached.

> *'But to those who have accepted him, he has given the power of becoming sons of God.*
> *Since these were born not of human stock or of flesh, but of God.'*
> (Jn 1:12–13)

That is a great day and I think that sooner or later it will come for all, not because we are more or less decent people, but because he, having the power to make us pull faces, will eventually succeed in getting us to say 'Father', since his loving will is constantly putting pressure on us and vigorously prompting us to do so.

The gestation of a child lasts for nine months. Our gestation as sons of God, a whole lifetime.

The child in its mother's womb has little room to dispose

of; in God's womb there is all the room in the world.

But even if we can run and do all sorts of other things in it, this is still 'inside', and hence we still can't see the face of our begetter.

'*In him, we are, we move, we breathe*' (Act 17:28), but we do not see.

When we eventually emerge, we shall see him face to face, as Scripture tells us.

Now, God wraps us up like this, and the darkness of his activity is called faith; the incentive to become our complete selves is called hope, and the love sustaining all this is called charity.

It is hard for us not to forget that he is there.

It is hard because everything happens in silence, and the silence frightens us.

We should like him to say, 'Here I am' or reveal his presence with thunder and lightning.

If he has occasionally done this, as Exodus relates, he did it because mankind was still a child and needed to be treated like one.

But he prefers silence.

He is silent now because this is more suitable to man's maturity.

God's silence is a sign of your maturity in faith. If it frightens you, this is because in some respects you are still a child.

Children are frightened by silence and the dark, but they have to get used to the one and the other.

The things of God have no need of words.

'*The heavens proclaim God's glory,*
the sky displays his creative skill;
day after day, this is re-attested,
night after night, this is re-affirmed.

Not by speaking, not by talking,
not by any sound that can be heard,
but, by spanning the entire earth,
this message reaches the whole world.'

(Ps 19:1–4)

Things speak for themselves; the heavens themselves speak.

But God comes in silence.

And this is why I do not believe much in apparitions connected with the Virgin, particularly in the sensational signs by which these manifest their presence.

I prefer to talk to our Lady in the monotone of the Rosary, with my eyes closed in hope.

Illusions frighten me.

I do not want my senses conditioning my relationship with the Invisible.

I know that the path of faith, hope and charity leads in the opposite direction from the path of illusion.

It leads towards God's silence.

Towards the starkness of the Cross.

Towards the transparency of night.

It is like light. In the cosmos all is dark, outside the atmosphere all is dark.

Yet nothing is more luminous than this pure darkness.

One of the commonest difficulties in the spiritual life of man today is this very crossing from hubbub into silence, from childishness into maturity of faith, from a surplus of statues to the starkness of the Eucharist, from preoccupation with self to charity, from sentimentality to aridity, from impressive processions to the poverty-ridden streets of the human city.

Faced with the harsh realities of demythologisation and secularisation, many Christians – too many – are positively terrified.

Accustomed to touching a statue and to kissing this and that, now that these have gone and the liturgical calendar has been modernised, they feel quite lost.

Where is God?

What on earth are things coming to, if that fool of a curate can put St George and the Dragon in the sacristy cupboard?

But the crisis is even worse as regards prayer.

I don't feel anything anymore!

I don't see anything anymore!

The Christianity we used to have was often conditioned by *feeling*. . . by *seeing*. Religion was based on emotion and the miraculous.

And our shrines seem to have been designed expressly to foster this kind of religiosity.

Now that the modern world, technology and social communications have destroyed myth, have revealed some things for the childishness they were, have demonstrated the laws of nature: everything collapses, everything dissolves.

I don't believe anymore, you hear people say.

But was it ever faith in the first place?

Yes, of course it was faith, but with a high admixture of superstition.

Take away the support of superstition and you are left with a faith so rickety that it can't go on standing up.

True faith does not need to feel: it believes.

Mature faith has no need to see: it believes.

It is nourished by silence, not by noise.

By contemplation, not by prodigies.

By the word of God, not by superstition.

Shall I then never feel anything of Him?

Must I wait for the lightning of the Apocalypse before I escape from the darkness?

Listen, I shall tell you what you ought to feel and see!

You should feel and see the creatures, every creature.

Why take such an interest in a dewdrop appearing on the Virgin's eyelash in a painting, yet not see all the dewdrops of a morning in spring?

Why go miles and miles to see the dubious stigmata on someone or other's hands, yet not move a step to contemplate the sore-covered hands of the poor?

Begin feeling God in creatures.

See his beauty in the beauty of the sun as it rises on your human day.

Hear his voice in the voice of the brother beside you, trying to communicate with you.

Waste no more time, seeking God in your own fantasies.

Once you realise how miraculous it is that a bee can find the door of its hive, you will feel that God is near you and near your silence.

Try and sing.

For the sky that you have given us, alleluia!

For the sun that you have given us, alleluia!

For the sea that you have given us, alleluia!

For the friends that you have given us, alleluia!

Yes, alleluia, even if the sky is sometimes stormy.

Alleluia, even if the sun is sometimes scorching.

Alleluia, even if your friends do not always see eye to eye with you.

All is grace.

All is God, loving me.

God is in all, moulding me.

God is in all, making me his son.

We can define our earthly life as '*life for two*'.

We are never alone if we live in Him.

We are never alone if God is in touch with us.

We are never alone if he is begetting us for his Kingdom.

The habit of feeling his presence within us shows great maturity.

The establishing of living communication with him in prayer is great sweetness.

The acceptance of his higher level than ours is true wisdom.

But acquiring this maturity and making this wisdom ours is not easy.

We are always tempted in conflicting directions: either, caught by his absolute immanence, we abandon ourselves to inaction, saying, '*Let him act*', or, made enthusiastic by our security, we act without thinking about his secret activity.

There was a time when the first of these temptations was the easier.

Nowadays, the second is the easy one.

Modern man supposes that he acts alone.

He has conceived the notion of the 'Incomplete', maintaining that God's creative activity ceased with the appearance of Man, and that Man's task henceforward is to complete the symphony left in draft by God.

It is an interesting thesis and may help many people to acquire a sense of responsibility, but it can also give rise to misunderstanding and is not really able to make things any the clearer.

I prefer to start from one of Christ's sayings, '*My Father goes on working, and so do I* ' (Jn 5:17).

These Gospel phrases sum up all the arguments old and new, ancient and modern, about the vital relationship between God and Man, between contemplation and action, and keep error at bay.

In saying, '*My Father goes on working, and so do I*', Jesus was not saying that he had been left to complete the symphony of his life on his own.

Indeed, elsewhere he says, '*I am always with Him. And He who has sent me is with me; he has not left me on my own, since I always do what pleases him*' (Jn 8:29).

The Father is never absent from Christ's life, and Jesus never takes a decision without first referring to the Father.

Modern man seems to have become so sure of himself, so full of his own knowledge, that he seriously believes that he is really completing the incomplete on his own.

Having made a few initial steps in discovering the nature of things, he supposes himself to have reached a point where sole and absolute responsibility for the cosmos is his.

God's silence – which in any case is eternal – is interpreted as God's death, that is to say, an attitude so utterly passive on his part that it is useless to call or cry or pray to him. He has decided to let man manage on his own.

No interpretation could be more mistaken or more dangerous to faith.

It would mean the death of prayer,

the abolition of dialogue between God and man,

and the reduction of earth to a very sorry place, since – let us not forget – '*we do not perceive God when he acts, but we shudder when he says nothing.*'

But coming back to man in his relationship to God and in his relationship to things requiring effort to achieve, to be done properly as they turn up in life from day to day –

Jesus says, '*My Father goes on working, and so do I*', clearly acknowledging the polarity of action.

He is at work, and the Father is at work, that is to say, man and God.

Both are at work.

In Christ's life, the Father's presence never fails.

Jesus doesn't hide this, doesn't forget this; he sees it. He doesn't run away from this; he seeks it.

I am not alone, because the Father is with me.

(Jn 16:32)

Father, I thank you for having heard me. I did indeed know that you always do hear me, but I said this for the sake of these people standing round me.

(Jn 11:42)

You need only read St John's Gospel through, to have a continuous, progressively amazing record of the life of intimacy, mutual understanding, hope, dialogue and love existing between Jesus and the Father.

Perhaps it would be different for man, for us? Perhaps Jesus wasn't the perfect man, the unique and primal exemplar?

What happened in Jesus happens or will happen in each of us, since he is the first-born and since the Father's love has decreed that all the living shall by adoption receive that same quality of first-born, becoming brothers in the fullest sense, immense multitudes redeemed by the blood of One who was willing to give his life to accomplish this loving design.

Yes, like Jesus.

And as Jesus is of the same mind as the Father, so we are to be in communion with the Father.

As Jesus conversed with the Father, so we are to converse with the Father.

There are two poles in this love and dialogue, and two there must remain.

Sin consists in suppressing one of the two.

If I leave man out of the equation and think that all is done by God, I err, but equally I err if I leave God out, thinking that I act alone.

And as regards this relationship between God and man, be it remembered that this is not a matter of hazy abstractions.

It concerns persons.

I am a person and God is a person.

Christian 'personalism' contemplated in the Trinity has always saved me from reducing the faith to something vague and evanescent.

The harder I have tried to advance towards intimacy with God, the more I have experienced the personal nature of God.

The Father is not the same person as Jesus, and when

Jesus says, '*My Father goes on working, and so do I*', he is making a clear statement, which I find very illuminating.

Wasn't Abraham listening to a person, when he heard the voice say, '*Leave your native land*' (Gn 12:1)?

Didn't Moses recognise a person in God's presence in the burning bush — '*Take off your shoes. . .* (Ex 3:5)?

Let only your will be done in me and in all your creatures

What God proposes to man in that lengthy period of gestation as son of God is the simplest thing you can imagine.

'While waiting for the Kingdom, make the Kingdom.

'While waiting to be my son, behave as a father.

'While waiting for righteousness and peace, practise righteousness and peace.

'While waiting for what you desire to be given you, give the same thing to your brothers.

'You want a paradise of love? – make earth a paradise.

'You want to be forgiven? – forgive.

'You want to have your hunger appeased? – appease.

'You want to be set free? – set free.'

And thus, for man, Earth becomes the experimental field for his desires, the actuation of what he has at heart, the experience in the visible of what he aspires to in the invisible.

In building the city, obstructed by his weakness and even more so by his ignorance as he is, man engages all his thirst for righteousness and goodness.

Mistakes notwithstanding, he is constantly urged forward by the idea of the Kingdom.

And even when things go completely wrong, he has at least got the guts to blazon his original intentions on the pediment of his structures: the ideals which had prompted him to act.

And where he has made a mistake, his sons will begin again, starting from their fathers' errors and doing their best to correct them.

Every generation has the sense of starting afresh, especially those that are the product of some appalling catastrophe or war.

Every revolutionary optimistically steps forward, his bright eyes affirming his conviction, 'Now I'll show you how it's done – you see!'

And everything begins again.

But all is not lost.

What genuinely remains is love.

What however are not always genuinely effective are institutions.

In people's wearisome efforts to stabilise their ideals and policies, institutions are the necessary and indeed indispensable repositories of what they have achieved to date.

Institutions may be home, college, seminary – to educate people; laws – to impose order on their relationships; customs, traditions, culture, town-council, state, parish, diocese, church.

But while love never grows old, institutions run the risk of growing old and, worse still, of surviving to clutter the ground and to scandalise people by their uselessness.

The seminary is still at such and such a number in such and such a street: but it is empty.

Law number such and such under section so and so of the constitution serves no purpose now, because customs have altered.

Let me give you an example from real life. Since the matter is a rather sensitive one, I shall try to be accurate.

The place is. . . The date is December 13, 1974. It will be Christmas in twelve days' time and this town has a particular devotion to the Christmas crib.

Two pilgrims arrive: Marie-Madeleine, French, 28, social worker, and Sandy, Canadian, 25, sociologist. They are bound for Rome, hoping to arrive there on foot for Christmas and the opening of the Holy Year.

They have no money in their pockets, since they want to

make the journey in a spirit of poverty and find out what happens when you are poor.

Having prayed in church, they go round all the convents and charitable institutions, looking for somewhere to spend the night.

Night falls and they still haven't found anywhere.

'Closed. . . closed. . . go round the corner. . . go up there. . . try down there.'

Deeply disgusted, the two leave the town and find a caravan in a field on the outskirts. Two Norwegian Protestants are on holiday. The foreigners come to an understanding and the caravan, small as it is, becomes the nightly refuge from the cold for four.

And that's the problem – terrible! A rickety caravan can discharge the duties of hospitality more effectively than a large, anonymous, loveless institution.

In the caravan, you get a personal welcome; in the big convent, in that massive block of bricks and mortar, the individual doesn't count. Instead, there are door-bells, gates, the rule, absolute peace and perfect order.

The institution has got the upper hand.

Man is crushed or excluded.

The poor man doesn't know where he ought to go.

There is no one in the institution to bother about him.

The same thing happened to Jesus.

The institution of the Temple was too ossified to welcome him.

Later, it was too deaf to understand him.

Finally, to get rid of him, it was willing to kill him.

But that isn't the whole story, for people of yesteryear were no worse than we are, as we by the same token are certainly no better than they were.

From Adam to the last man on earth, things will not change.

There will always be doors that open, and doors that shut.

There will be men like the Good Samaritan, and others like Dives.

There will be men like Gamaliel who try to save the innocent, and others like Caiaphas who will find a good reason for putting them to death.

I used to imagine that what happened under the Old Covenant could not be repeated under the New, and that the mistakes of the Temple would never recur in the Church founded by Jesus.

I was grossly mistaken, and for a long while the mistake prevented me from coming to grips with reality.

No, brothers.

There is a fragment of the Temple in each of us; a bit of that institution's wall still clutters everyone's heart.

The coming of Jesus did not make his Church a Church of Saints; it left it a Church of sinners.

Laying an even greater responsibility on these sinners for having brought them nearer to God's great light, which shone with such brilliance with the coming of Jesus on earth.

Even so, man is still man, with all his wonderful potentialities for love, as well as his capacity for refusing love.

And the Church is still the Church, with all its immense reservoir of holiness, as well as its weakness and capacity for getting out of date.

Temple and Gospel will always, until the end of time, be capable of heroic, indeed divine, achievement, but nonetheless will be the source of strife and scandal.

On the selfsame day, a pilgrim in Rome can be edified and scandalised by one and the same acquaintance.

And that acquaintance could well be us.

———————

But salvation will ever be in the Gospel.
The Gospel is what counts.

When institutions begin to weigh me down, when I feel I am no longer being true to myself, I must forthwith seek freedom, suppleness and directness in the Gospel.

I cannot do without institutions; I need them but must fine them down, must make them apt to serve man, not themselves to be served.

Institutions are the armour in which Saul tries to dress David.

It is David's business to decide whether it is useful, or whether he should reduce his burden to a sling.

The Gospel will always tell you when you need the armour, and when the sling alone.

But here I ought to offer a word of warning to those who, having taken David's sling, see in their newfound freedom the best method for fighting the spiritual combat.

Some go so far as only to feel free when they stop referring their actions to the Church; others only feel they are being true to themselves once they have relegated their relationship with God to the past and become involved in serving man without reference to tradition.

There is really no need for such clean breaks, especially since they divorce us from the truth.

The Church is still the Church, God is still God.

David is still the son of his people, and God is still the strength of his sling.

Who am I, if divorced from the People of God, and what strength is left in me, if faith in the Most High has failed?

The Church doesn't deny me the right to live as the Gospel says I should, and my commitment to God is all the more needful, now that I have decided to do something in earnest.

In the past, I know, religious life was all too often synonymous with, '*We don't want a fuss, please behave, we mustn't rock the boat, we must stay on the safe side*', but I also know that things have changed and that the word of God has started challenging and questioning us about righteousness and love, rather than about processions and vast programmes of church-building.

Why should I abandon the Church at the very moment when I feel myself more Church?

Why should we abandon God's inspiration at the very moment when we need it most?

Why think that God is most remote from us at the very moment when we become more closely committed to man?

Isn't God on man's side?

Isn't he the one to spring to man's defence?

Read St Matthew's Gospel and then tell me if you can find stronger words than those in Chapter 25 in defence of righteousness and the liberation of man?

I think that even Communists will realise their mistake of having regarded religion as the opiate of the people; and I also think that in tomorrow's world the men most determined to take the side of man will come from the ranks of the people still able – though selfishness be everywhere triumphant – to refer to the Gospel as the word of life.

And one last word about those who maintain the primacy of action and who mistrust prayer as alienation or waste of time.

Before all, action is obedience. '*With sweat on your brow shall you eat your bread*' (Gn 3:19).

A vocation. '*The Lord chose me from my mother's womb to bring the glad news*' (cf. Is 61:1).

A passion for good. '*And when he saw the crowds he felt sorry for them, because they were harassed and dejected, like sheep without a shepherd*'(Mt 9:36).

This is why we act.

Since he has told us to act.

To put action and contemplation in opposition to one another is therefore an absurdity.

Man makes, acts, works, transforms, builds – out of

obedience, not in opposition, to the will of God.

The mystery lies in the relationship.

And this is a living relationship.

It is a relationship between presences.

It is a communicating relationship.

Yes, I act because God has commanded me to do so.

He commanded me in Genesis, ordering me to till and produce order on earth.

He commanded me on Sinai, giving me a law to act righteously; he commanded me in the Gospel, involving me in the very activity of God: love.

Work, righteousness, love are three degrees of commitment and the three ways available for man in building the earthly city as concrete sign of and immediate preparation for the heavenly city, eventually achieving it under God's transforming touch : '*I make all things new*' (Rv 21:5).

But whether in the manual work of dealing with a field, ploughing and sowing the seed, or in giving judgment in the law courts, or in setting up a hospital for lepers, I do not act alone. God is with me, as Jesus says, '*My Father has not left me on my own*' (cf. Jn 8:16).

God is with me as inspiration.

God is with me as grace.

God is with me as strength.

God is with me as light.

God is with me as talent.

God is with me as reproof.

And his presence is not theoretical.

His presence is not evanescent.

His presence is not sterile.

His presence is personal, vital and fruitful.

That same presence as in the creation.

And this presence is what I have to wonder about.

This is always the real problem of faith: from Adam to Jesus, from Jesus to us.

'*The Father is in me and I am in him*'.

As a person.

Being a person means seeing, knowing, loving, wishing; it means communicating.

And what doubts can our faith entertain when the whole 'Word' tends to demonstrate it?

Isn't this the very mystery hidden throughout the centuries of the Old Dispensation, handed down to us by the prophets and confirmed for us by Christ?

If not so, why did Yahweh say to David, '*I shall be his Father and he will be my son*' (2 S 7:14)? and to Solomon, '*I give you a wise and shrewd heart. Furthermore, I shall give you what you have not asked me for: riches and honour*' (1 K 3:12–13)?

And faced with sick Hezekiah's plea, doesn't God reply, '*I have heard your prayer and tears; I shall cure you and in three days' time you will go up to the Temple of Yahweh*' (2 K 20–5)?

And when Isaiah was trying to express his prophetic hope, didn't he say, '*Yahweh called me before I was born, before my birth he had pronounced my name. He made my mouth a sharp sword and hid me in the shadow of his hand. He made me into a sharpened arrow and concealed me in his quiver, saying to me, "You are my servant, Israel, through whom I shall manifest my glory"*' (Is 49:1–3)?

If from the Bible and particularly from the Gospel you exclude this mode of being, this personal relationship between God and man, you completely abandon Tradition, the plain sense of the Word.

And experience of God too!

The nearer you come to him in contemplation, the more you discover him as root of your action, author of your vocation, inspirer of your prophetic faculty, giver of your special talents.

The more you pray, the more you feel the distance growing between him and you, and this indicates the ever-sharper distinction between him as person and you as person.

The further you penetrate the silence, the more you feel

yourself dwelt in by the Word.

The more you penetrate creatures in the harmony of love, the more you discover him to be present and distinct from creatures in the mystery of his transcendence.

'You' becomes the nearest and most experienced of words.

The need to make room for this 'You' is one of life's continuous demands.

I wish no more than this, O Lord

'You', what an amazing word you are!

'You', what an irrefutable sign of communication!

When I utter you, I come out of my loneliness and isolation.

You designate my brother, friend, bride, father.

If you can designate my God, there are no limits to communication.

Being able to say 'You' in spirit and truth to God himself can change the face of the world: it certainly changes my life.

This 'You' is the soul of prayer.

'O God my God, I pine for you,
how thirsty my soul is for you,
my body longing more for you
than arid ground for drops of moisture!'

(Ps 63:1)

It is the symbol of the Other and favourite theme.

'Compared with the skies created by your fingers
and the moon and stars fixed by you in space,
what is man, for you to spare a thought for him?
a human being, for you to care for him?'

(Ps 8:3–4)

It is the summons to faith.

'All things look to you
to give them food when they need it;

when you give, they gather,
when you open your hand, they fill up, O Good One!'

(Ps 104:27–28)

The fabric of the dialogue.

'Should I stray like a lost sheep, look for your servant!
For I have not forgotten your commandments.'

(Ps 119:176)

The experience of God's nearness summed up in a word.

'Your hands have made and moulded me:
give me insight to learn your commandments!'

(Ps 119:73)

We can never define what prayer is.
Words are not enough for us.
No saint has succeeded in doing it.
Prayer so far exceeds all definition as always to leave room for a mystery.
Yes, prayer is a mystery.
Praying is communicating with the mystery called God.
Try it yourself and you will see, however skilful you are, that you will not succeed in putting your experience of prayer into words.
But one aspect of it you will certainly be able to define, when you say that it is a relationship between two persons.
When you pray, you will feel yourself in the presence of Someone Else.
Maybe you feel the Someone Else inside you.
Maybe you feel him outside you.
Maybe you feel enveloped in him.
Maybe he feels far, far away from you.
Maybe you feel him as Silence,
as Absence,

as Aridity,
as Darkness or as Light
or as Joy or as Fulness
or as Reproof.

There are no limits to the way in which we experience God.

He is always new, and I suspect that he never repeats himself in the way he chooses to approach us.

When I was waiting for him under the olive-tree, he came under the oak.

When I was waiting for him in church, he came in the city.

When I sought him in joy, he came in sorrow.

When I gave up waiting for him I found him before me, waiting for me.

God has always taken me by surprise, and his time has never been mine.

If I had to tell you how I try to dispose myself – for I do not always succeed – when I pray, I should quote you Psalm 131, one of the loveliest and one with which I feel very much in tune.

> '*Yahweh, my heart is not haughty,*
> *my eyes are not raised unduly high.*
> *I have not meddled with lofty matters*
> *or busied myself with wonders above my head,*
> *but have kept my soul even and tranquil*
> *like an infant with its mother –*
> *like an infant with Him is my soul.*'

Yes, like an infant, but very much an infant, a something with something of the foetus still about it: the inability to make long speeches, I might even say, the inability to speak at all.

Don't you find when you pray that you usually don't know what to say?

That's it, this is already true prayer.

Having a clear awareness of not knowing God's

language, or hardly knowing how to stammer out a few syllables, and then relapsing into silence: this is true experience of prayer.

Though of course, this foetus, this baby, is still enveloped in Adam's flesh, wearing an old man's mask over its face.

Those who do talk, talk too much, as Jesus remarked, '*In your prayers do not babble as the pagans do, for they think that by using many words they will make themselves heard*' (Mt 6:7). But what they say is not so much prayer as spiritual gossip: often a cultural display, or even more often fear.

But when the babe, the babe of God inside each of us about to become a son of God, when he prays he doesn't say much, because he doesn't know what to say.

Instead of talking, he '*lies down*' and '*sleeps*', he '*lets things happen*', '*he senses that he is enveloped in God*', he has '*confidence*'.

For the one praying in him is that same Love which is begetting him, the Spirit of the Father dwelling in him and accustoming him little by little to saying, '*My Father and my God*'.

Many words are not necessary, instead the Word is necessary and with this we can always pray when of ourselves we can say nothing.

What matters is to let Him act in us, for he is *Life* and transmits life to us,

he is *Light* and transmits his own knowledge,

he is *Love* and teaches us to love.

True prayer – that which abides and is effective – is contemplation, and this is passive, being impressed by God on his child so that the latter may come to know his father and grow accustomed to loving him, as the first commandment requires.

'*You are to love God with all your heart, with all your soul, with all your strength*' (Dt 6:5), with your whole self.

Now perhaps you will have grasped why I have been insisting on the divine truth that God makes 'sons' of us.

Sons, not pictures.

Sons, not dragonflies.

Sons, not tables.

Sons, not slaves.

On this fact of being sons is based the ability to pray, the possibility of communicating, the joy of loving.

If I were not a son of God, prayer would have no meaning and, what is more, would serve no purpose.

If prayer is communicating with God, this is possible if God makes me share his own nature.

Paradise means something to me if I am going to live with my father, not with some being whom I do not and shall never know, with different tastes from mine, with a language unintelligible and a face invisible to me.

I know that God is the *unknowable*, but he is that for me as 'man', not for me as '*his son*'.

His *unknown-ness* becomes known, not in my human intellect, but in the power which he has given me to be his son.

In the love which he exerts to beget me as his son, he transmits knowledge of him as Father to me.

When God reveals himself to me in love, he makes me a gift of himself and makes me know him personally.

This is called contemplation, which is true, savoury, personal knowledge of God.

Yes, I say this because I can say this, '*I believe in God because I know him*'.

The old man in me believes in God only by analogy, through nature, reason and symbols; but the 'babe' of God, born and enveloped in me, believes in God because he knows him.

And knows him because he makes himself known. But not in flesh and blood – in the same divine life which he transmits in his love.

This is my strength.

And in this strength I put my hope.

In this extraordinary fact, I rejoice throughout my life.

———————

One last thing.

When I affirm in faith that God is my father, I throw a light divine on another great mystery: the mystery of mind.

How sublime mind is!

How fine a thing in us!

That such kingly dignity should dwell in this frail being, man!

I think of mind as the place where Abraham meets Yahweh;

as the Valley of the Terebinth, where David sought the pebbles to launch at Goliath;

as Horeb for Elijah;

as the little room where Mary of Nazareth received the annunciation;

as the wilderness and as Gethsemane for Jesus.

The mind is the divine environment of man.

It is the possibility of meeting with his God.

It is listening to his Word.

The crucible where faith becomes life, where hope matures and love is perfected.

If God, in making man's body, copied stars and flowers, in making my mind, he copied himself at that point where the Divine Persons meet in Love.

For me as son of man, the mind is the lantern to my steps,

for me as son of God, the mind is the home where the Father takes me in his arms and says, 'You are my little boy.'

When I enter it, I take off my shoes, for I am in his presence.

When I stay in it, I hear the breathing of my God as he looks for me.

The mind is the masterpiece of God's creation,

it is the terrain on which he meets us,

it is our intimacy with him,
the place where the truth makes headway, where his will is sought, where we learn to love.

There, in my mind I find all that I know about God; and there, I make my decisions.

The very decision to believe in the infallibility of the Church, I make in my mind.

Without reference to it, as far as I am concerned, there is no moral act worthy of God or done for God.

I believe in the mind and should like to see Christians, too long used to the convenience of relying on other men's guidance, begin – and seriously at that – to be guided by their own minds, these having been given by God.

It is time for us to stop shutting ourselves behind inflated scruples based on the idea that the mind makes a dangerous guide because, being insufficiently enlightened, it is liable to make mistakes.

Keep calm.

If I believe that God is my father, I can put such fears out of my head and put my trust in his love and in his ability to communicate his thought and will to me.

A Church which once perhaps needed to insist – and how zealously she did so! – on controlling her members' minds, today, after the toils of the last ten years and pervaded by the light of the Council, need only sing for joy at the marvels attendant on the fact that man can converse directly with God.

PART TWO

If God is my father
I am his son

To understand what
being his son means
we have to look at the First-born Son
Jesus.

He came to us
he dwelt among us
living his adventure
as Son of God –
the Christ

Imitating Christ
is hence the way for us.

Into your hands I commend my soul

To meet me, God made himself poor in Jesus, and thus his poverty became the sign of his love for me.

He had no other way of making himself credible.

Love makes terrible demands and, to satisfy these, words are not enough.

Anyone in love has to become like the beloved, or the latter will pass by without noticing, that is to say, without returning love.

To be drawn to someone means having the strength to 'suffer', to sympathise, with him; means having something in common.

This isn't easy, but there is no other way and this is why it is difficult to love.

Can you imagine a husband claiming to love his wife yet leaving her to starve while he is rich, to wear herself out while he sits idle, to weep while he laughs?

How can one brother claim to love another, when the latter is hungry and the former well-fed, while the latter is naked and the former well-dressed, while the latter is in prison and the former free?

Can that be called playing fair?

Wouldn't it be more honest to say outright, '*I don't love you*', or '*I haven't the strength to love you*', or, what would be even truer, '*I should like to love you, but am not capable of doing so*'?

The world is full to overflowing with talk of love, but is virtually void of true love, I believe.

Apart from man, no animal on earth feigns love to hoodwink its own kind.

Even those wild beasts, those classed as the most savage, are angels in comparison with man with his capacity for lapping up this counterfeit relationship known as love.

Go into a brothel – and a great many middleclass homes are no less – and see the degree to which a woman can be enslaved by her protector and owner who, since tough, or rich, or influential, can always dupe her by murmuring the well-worn refrain, 'I love you' in her ears.

Go to Vietnam and count the craters made by super-bombers controlled by people who claim to be fighting in defence of and for love of free peoples.

But God is more honest, and when he says that he loves man, he goes the whole way and, to love him, takes flesh and, to be like him, becomes poor.

God's poverty is God's way of loving.

There is however one difference between God's poverty and man's.

God's poverty is freely chosen; man's poverty is an inexorable condition, his nature, his reality.

Man cannot get away from his poverty.

Man is, by definition, poor.

A limited, materialistic notion of poverty has long made people regard poverty as a physical condition, as a lack of food, clothing, housing.

A poor man is a beggar.

But man's poverty is more than this.

True, anyone who has nowhere to live and nothing to eat is poor, but there are other kinds of poor people too.

There are far worse types of human poverty, more fearful forms of penury, more acute sorts of suffering.

Hemingway wasn't short of food or clothing. He even owned a hunting rifle, which he often used on his African safaris.

Eventually, he used it to fire a bullet into his own mouth and so escape the real poverty tormenting him, perhaps when he first became aware of it: the for him intolerable poverty of old age.

Why see poverty as a merely physical phenomenon? Isn't that unduly circumscribed?

It may be that someone doesn't ask me for a salary rise, but pleads for a little peace, a breath of fresh air, a bit of greenery.

No, poverty isn't merely lack of money.

It can be lack of health, of fresh air, of peace of mind.

It can be lack of peace, love, light.

You can say that man's poverty is all-embracing. You can go further and say that man is poverty personified.

Not because he lacks a bit of food, but because he lacks everything.

When he hates, he lacks love.

When he dies, he lacks life.

Yes, man's poverty is very death and that is no light thing; that is one thing he cannot send packing when it knocks on his door.

Yet precisely on this path of poverty is where God comes to meet us.

The free poverty of God sits down beside the forced poverty of man.

And silent is their opening conversation.

What can be said to someone who is suffering?

God's silence is a mark of his respect as he approaches poor humanity.

The time for saying things hasn't come yet.

He wants to give man time to understand his plight, to raise his head and smile, despite the flood of ills assailing him.

A blind woman once told me it had taken her twelve years to come to terms with her blindness.

Then she grasped the point, and smiled.

There is a mystery in things.

There is a mystery in life.

There is a mystery in pain.

It is like darkness, and to see we have to wait until dawn.

And waiting means hoping, and hope is human patience.

And it is precisely in this patience that man learns to possess and know himself.

Indeed, as Scripture says, '*In patience you will possess your souls*' (Lk 21:19).

Once man has learnt patience and grown used to waiting for God's silence, he becomes the Word.

The Word, the whole Word is Jesus, the person of Jesus, the Word of God.

'*And the Word was made flesh
and he lived among us*' (Jn 1:14)

and he lived among us as a poor man.

The poor man of Yahweh.

He willed to take man's poverty on himself, to help him complete the terrible exodus marked by poverty, suffering and death.

Jesus's whole life is to be seen in this light, was to be lived in this context and directed to this end.

He was born in a stable and his infinite omnipotence was reduced to the whimpering of a babe at the mercy of history and human wickedness; and this was to teach us life's hardest lesson – to prepare us for the frailty and impotence of things.

He was concealed in the dough of the world; he accepted, not the honours of power, but the sweat of the working-man; and this was to accustom himself and to accustom us to the sweat of the death-agony.

As his law of conduct, he chose mildness, not violence; and this was because Divine Wisdom desires us to triumph, not by force, but by love, and that he should be victorious through the torments of the Cross.

For pattern, already refined by the prophets, he took the Servant of Yahweh, the Innocent One: a pattern embodying in deepest manner the hopes and spirituality of

Israel. And this was because he knew that the Kingdom, the true Kingdom of God, was not to be a political kingdom, powerful, stable and prosperous, but the greatest act of love of which God is capable here-below: acceptance of human poverty and death, the latter to be pledge of and crossing to fuller life.

It is not easy to love, either for us, or for Christ, but there is no greater thing than this; and it is brought to perfection by the way Jesus loved by willingly assuming and loving his poverty.

Nothing, nothing is dearer to me than this, God's poverty.

It is sweeter to me than his omnipotence.

It speaks clearer to me than his omniscience.

It is nearer to me than his beauty.

God's poverty – this is the highest degree of love.

His own beatitude now becomes mine: '*Blessed are the poor*'.

No, Lord, I shan't ask you again to make me rich; I ask you to make me poor.

I shan't ask you again for your power! I shall ask you for your poverty.

This is your wisdom.

This is your heart.

This is the road which leads you to me.

If you can bring yourself to approach me, sinner as I am, this is because you willed to be poor.

If you are prepared to stay and listen when I weep, this is because you are poor.

If you seek something in me, this is because you are poor.

Your poverty is what saves me since, in your poverty, Incarnate Love was able to become man and become a poor man like us.

———————

Where Jesus's poverty is most profound, most truly part

of the mystery of God's love, is in his obedience to the Father.

Faced with man's poverty, faced with evil, faced with the flood of pain, he did not ask the Father to alter things.

He saw that it was necessary to pass through this, and bowed his head like one of us.

He could have asked for death to be abolished: he did not ask.

He could have asked for Earth to be transformed into an Eden, where no one would ever be hungry again: he did not do so.

He could, he the Omnipotent, the Well-Beloved, have himself abolished pain and not endured it himself: he did not ask for this.

The real, the whole reality of the creation, made by God and corrupted by human disobedience and sin, had to be accepted as it was.

He had to start from this.

To accept it as the way of redemption.

To accept it as Calvary.

To accept it as a mystery.

To accept it as supreme self-giving.

Jesus bowed his head and accepted reality, gripping him like a deadly vice – a horrendous chaos suffocating him like an octopus.

And, under the pressure of all this evil, becoming the truly Poor Man of Yahweh, he plunged head first into the huge, mysterious sea of God's will – prefigured by Jonah – abandoning the solution of the insoluble and the synthesis of all opposites to God, the God of the Impossible.

And the Father accepted this obedience which heals all acts of disobedience, this abasement which cancels all acts of rebellion, this righteous action *'fulfilling all righteousness'* (Mt 3:15).

'And because of his humility, God heard him.'

(Heb 5:7)

'And because of his death, God raised him high and gave him the name which is above all other names.'

(cf. Ph 2:8–9)

And raised him from the dead.

Christ's resurrection is God's reply to human poverty, poverty absolutely accepted by Jesus.

The fish, having plunged into the infinite sea of God's will, down into the very abyss of death, rises by the impulsion of the Father's power into the boundless light of the Resurrection.

In the Risen Christ, man rises too.

Forever.

The secret of salvation lies in this attitude of acceptance, seen in Jesus, and lived by each of us, saved from the waters and from the chaos of death.

This was the secret hidden through the centuries and revealed to us in the fulness of time by Jesus.

This was the final proof that God is Love and that he was willing to die for love.

'Into your hand I commend my soul.'

These words from Father de Foucauld's prayer of abandonment boldly express this fundamental attitude as taught us by Jesus and enjoined on us in baptism.

Yes, the baptism preached by Christ is the deliberate action of man in response to God's request, *'Be drowned in the waters of death, to rise again to new life with Christ.'*

He who deliberately performs this act of acceptance of God's will, he who closes his eyes to his Transcendence and allows himself to be drawn into the mysterious abyss, will rise high, high, into the blissful light of very resurrection in Christ.

At such times, poverty truly becomes bliss.

'*Blessed are the poor, for theirs is the Kingdom of Heaven*' (cf. Lk 6:20).

How could Jesus have said anything so bold and authoritative to the poor, unless by the light of this divine truth henceforth to be shared by saved mankind?

The words '*Blessed are the poor, Blessed are those who mourn, Blessed are the hungry, Blessed are the persecuted*' would sound outrageous to anyone who is poor, who is hungry, who is mourning, who is persecuted, did these not express Christ's victory over these fearful negative realities.

The words of Jesus would sound absolutely insane if, in uttering them, he had not had a clear vision of the whole problem of how man was to be set free.

But to be free, we have to die to ourselves. That is the Passover.

'*This is the Passover, when the Lamb is sacrificed.*

This is the night when you freed our forefathers from slavery in Egypt.

This is the night which saves us from the darkness of evil, when you overcame the darkness of sin.

This is the night when Christ, destroying death, rises victorious from the underworld.

O truly blessed night,
O night defeating evil,
wiping away our guilt,
leading man back to his God!
O wonderful condescension of his grace!
O inestimable tenderness of his love!
To redeem the slave
He has sacrificed the Son.
Happy the guilt warranting such a redeemer!
Had it not been for Adam's sin,
Christ would not have redeemed us.
Happy the guilt warranting such a redeemer!'

And I should like to add:

*Happy our poverty
since it has power
to draw us to you,
our God!*

I offer it to you

Giving my life to you, Lord, means accepting yours.
Giving my soul to you, Lord, means accepting yours.
And your soul is still in Gethsemane with our poverty.
And your life is still nailed to the cross by our sin.

My life, if led remote from the vision, remote from the reality which you have lived and which you live in your Body, the Church, is a useless, pagan life, a prey to delusion, weariness and death.

Yet, if I put my trust only in your resurrection, if I byepass your Gethsemane and Cross, it would be dangerous, as this is mankind's Gethsemane and cross too.

If I think only of your incarnation, without accepting mine, I reduce your existence and mine to a blasphemous farce.

No, Jesus, if I give you my soul and my life, I am at the centre of your soul and of your life. And you are at the centre of your Mystical Body, the Church.

As long as there is one hungry man on earth, you are there.

As long as there is one man suffering on earth, you are there.

As long as there is one man to be set free, you are there.
And if I want to be with you, I have to be with man.
There is no way round this.
I cannot deceive myself about this.

And anyhow, I should not want to do so, once having understood this.

And I feel solidarity with these new-wave Christians who have understood this.

Beside my mourning brother, let me mourn.

Beside the prisoner, let me stay in prison.

I cannot accept resurrection, unless I first accept death.

The Easter mystery is not only about the resurrection, is not only the joy of Easter Sunday.

Primarily it is about the painful solidarity of Good Friday.

How unworthy of love – true love, I mean – to want to rejoice alone with Christ!

How unfair to crowd into his banquet, yet leave him alone to his sorrow and revulsion in the Garden of Olives!

It is so unfair that, in our more lucid moments, we should rather not accept paradise, without first – weak as we are – sharing something of his Passion.

Who could resist him – the Man of Sorrows?

Who that loves him, that is?

This is why the delights of this world, of 'this house of pleasures' as the pagans conceive it, repel me.

It is like feasting over a corpse.

Life regarded solely as pleasure, is not life; it is a brothel.

It is not worthy of Love.

I do not want it.

Who did lead a life worthy of love is Jesus.

And Jesus it is who teaches me how to love.

Jesus it is who gives me the strength to do it.

Jesus is the way.

And the way pursued by him is the way of Love.

Before being the way of resurrection, it is the way of abjection, of abandonment; before triumph, it is defeat and crucifixion.

I wish to pursue this way to the end, cost what it may.

Yes, the way is Jesus.

And our way is to imitate his.

To imitate Jesus!

Imitating him above all in his attitude to the Father; imitating him by accepting reality.

Whatever surrounds me, whatever is, whatever forms the
fabric of the creation, of history, whatever is the result of
God's design or of my past trangressions: this I have to
accept.

I have to start from here.

If I am lame, I have to accept being lame.

If I am tired, I have to accept being tired.

If skies are grey, I have to accept grey skies.

Whatever is, whatever surrounds me,

whatever I see, whatever I feel,

is like a mysterious demand incessantly made on me by
God, who is waiting for me to respond.

That terrible demand made on Job on his dunghill was
put to him by God.

'My son has polio,

'my wife is unbearable',

'I am slow on the uptake',

'my friends don't understand me'

are so many demands made on me throughout each daw-
ning day I have to live.

I cannot bury my son in some faceless institution,

I can't change wives,

I can't put the blame on my father, who was an alcoholic,
or quarrel with my superiors.

I have to look reality in the face, I have to accept my sur-
roundings, I have to see reality as a demand by God.

Yes, I have to say, 'Father!'

I have to start from here.

I have to respond to God's demand put to me in that
painful reality – truly a dark mystery – and in it, actually in
it, discover my salvation.

For my salvation is contained in this demand.

If I get rid of my son because he takes up too much of my
time, I am running away.

If I change wives because the one I have upsets me, I am
running away.

Salvation, all salvation, is contained in my accepting my

mystery and, in it, the mystery of my wife and son.

There is a reason for everything.

Love's first attitude towards the creation is to accept the creation, even if it seems strange, incomplete and sometimes hostile, to me.

There is a reason for everything.

Even Job's sufferings have a reason.

Even my polio stricken son has a reason.

Even David's sin has a reason.

Even the destruction of Jerusalem has a reason.

But before trying to free myself from the suffering that has befallen me, before taking my son to the hospital, before making any effective move to correct the evil surrounding me, I have to bow my head before the mystery, I have to put myself in the same attitude as Christ and take his words as mine, '*Lord, let your will be done, not mine*' (Lk 22:42).

Basically, this is an attitude of confidence in God, and on this very confidence my relationship with him is based.

I know that God is Lord of the universe and that in his hands '*are all the depths of the underworld*'.

I know that God can do everything and that men and nations '*are as drops of water in a sieve and as dust in the scales*' (Is 40:15).

God is God, and no one conquers him.

And if he lets himself be conquered, it is only the better to conquer.

And if he lets evil triumph for a little while, this is only so that he can the more clearly confound it before our short-sighted eyes.

Trusting in God is putting all things into his invincible hands.

Is believing that the cosmos is inexorably ruled by his creative power.

Is hoping for the final victory of man, when he and all

history will obey the saving love of Him who is absolute Love.

If I curse the rain soaking me and the cold freezing my fingers,

if I lose hope because I am old or because of an illness giving me pain, I shall never penetrate the mystery of God.

If I cannot read the brilliance of the stars, if I walk past the sea without being aware of it, I do not grasp the mystery of God.

If I complain about everything,

if I find men a nuisance,

if I lose my temper because the soup tastes nasty,

if I shout because the children are playing in the garden,

if I scowl at anyone who rings my doorbell,

I am an old man with nothing left worth saying.

Trusting God.

Accepting reality.

Accepting it as God's saving will for me.

Accepting it to transform it by love and patience.

In a hermitage near mine lives a fair-haired mother with her son.

Every so often, the woman comes to ask me to help her, and brings her son with her.

But the son suffers from Down's syndrome and absorbs the woman's whole life and energy.

When I first met her, years ago, she asked me for advice about putting her son into an institution; it seemed the most sensible thing to do.

Each time I came home from visiting that sort of place, I was appalled.

How could I bear to see poor little Andrew disappear into one of those horrible wards of identical invalids?

'No, Marcella, Andrew should stay with you; you should be his life.'

Marcella's answer was to say nothing.

Then she asked for a hermitage, to try and fill that silence with prayer.

'Marcella, try and say something to God.'

'I can't. If I were to ask him for anything, it would only be for him to take this terrible burden away.'

'Try again.'

As she went away, she said, 'Brother Charles, isn't there really a suitable institution for Andrew?'

She came back on other occasions.

'Marcella, try and say something to God.'

'I should like to say, "May your will be done", but I still haven't got the strength. You say it for me. . .'

And now Marcella is the one who says '*May your will be done*' and, having finally managed to say it in faith, this has rid her of fear.

Now it would seem unnatural to her to hand her son over to the care of others.

It is as though she has given birth to him anew.

So what does the rest matter?

Her salvation begins here.

Her child has become a sacred trust.

And the gentleness of her expression?

Even at a distance she instructs me, when I think of this woman trying to do God's will.

A will expressed in the reality, the terrible reality surrounding her.

And perhaps Don Milani only began to be Don Milani, the true prophet of our times, once he began to accept the reality which God had prepared for him.

And prepared subject to every human limitation.

A huddle of tumbledown houses marooned on a piece of waste ground.

A small group of boys with neither interests nor talents.

But it was ordained that a little love should be injected into this poverty – with faith.

I think Don Milani has managed to say stranger, truer, more eternal things to our generation through this handful of nothingness, than he would have done, had his Cardinal made him dean of Florence Cathedral or even appointed him his Auxiliary Bishop.

With all the love in my heart

The choice made by Jesus was man, to love man.

It was the same as God's eternal choice: to take man's part.

God even took Cain's part after his horrible crime when he risked being killed in the subsequent blood-feud.

'Anyone who kills Cain is to suffer vengeance sevenfold'.
'Yahweh put a mark on Cain lest anyone running into him should kill him' (Gn 4:15).

God is on the sinner's side, because he is on man's side and man is a sinner.

Man's sin does not nullify God's hope.

God knows that man will come back, will repent, will understand.

God's faith in man is indestructable.

He is prepared to wait to the very end.

He knows that man's negative element will eventually become positive, that immaturity will become maturity, sin grace, hardness gentleness, darkness light, flight return, cruelty regret, aversion embrace.

Jesus told the parable of the prodigal son with each of us in mind, knowing that each of us would live our individual version of the story.

And he loves us as we are, at whatever stage of our journey.

He loves the potentiality in us.

The potentiality for conversion, return, love, light.

He loves the Magdalen when she is still a sinner, because

he already sees her gradual progress towards the light as
something marvellous, as something worth serious attention here on earth.

He loves Zacchaeus the sinner, robber, exploiter, and
finds it good that such a man can be capable of reversing his
conduct and becoming a friend to the poor.

Yes, God loves what in man is not yet.

What has still to come to birth.

What we love in a man is what already is: virtue, beauty,
courage, and hence our love is self-interested and fragile.

God, loving what is not yet and putting his faith in man,
continually begets him, since love is what begets.

By giving man confidence, he helps him to be born, since
love is what helps us to emerge from our darkness and
draws us to the light.

And this is such a fine thing to do that God invites us to
do the same.

The charity which he transmits to us is this very ability to
love things in a brother which do not as yet exist in him.

For me to love my brother's negative element is dis-
interested love.

To love him in his poverty, in his lies, in his impurity, in
his duplicity, in his darkness.

And love, swooping down on him, has the power to
regenerate him.

Love creates the divine environment for man, making
transformation possible.

By feeling himself loved, he is prompted to set out on the
way of salvation.

His poverty shrivels up, his lies become odious to him, his
impurity becomes a yearning for purity, his darkness is in-
vaded by light.

When Jesus tells me, '*Love your enemy*', he indicates the
maximum possibility and capacity for loving; and the same
time he offers me the maximum hope of having peace on
earth. By besieging my enemy with love and not with
weapons, I facilitate in him and in myself the possibility of

seeing that day dawn when '*calf and lion-cub will feed together and a child will put his hand into the viper's lair, and none will harm the other*' (cf. Is 11:6–9).

By my exertions, I expand the Kingdom promised us and enter my heritage of peace.

Yes, loving the negative in man.

Loving it in the certainty that tomorrow the positive will prevail.

Seen like this, the world no longer frightens me.

Seeing the city like this, I feel a hearty desire to act and to hope.

Before I understood these things, sin filled me with repulsion; I thought of it as an enemy.

By the same token, I felt friendly towards the police who arrested prostitutes, and willingly preached on the perils of hell-fire to frighten the lads – to put the fear of God in them.

But now the sinner fills me with compassion; if I run into a prostitute I offer her a coffee; I have more hope in salvation, and the compassion which I feel for the sufferings of mankind is so intense that I utter the word 'hell' far less often.

You might say – and this gives me intense and heart-felt joy – that I feel myself a friend to all, I am no longer upset when I meet someone who doesn't believe in God, I am more surprised when the opposite occurs; I cannot not belong to a sinful Church.

When I run into some 'right-minded' person of the old moralising type, I realise how the Church's slow progress is due to lack of confidence in the coming generations, and to the assumption that the old days exemplified the only way in which things should be done.

Yes, loving the negative in man, loving what is not yet in him.

Those who have 'given up all hope' for Christianity are

precisely those who only want to see the positive in man and set no value on the negative.

This is why they suffer.

How could they not suffer at the sight of such disorder.

I admit it: the world is a terrible sight today if only seen in the light of what goes on: if not seen in the light of our hope that God overcomes evil.

The city seen from its positive side represents God's defeat.

The Church seen from the same point of view looks as though she's done for.

But seeing things like this and talking of them like this, I basically deny God's mysterious activity: he acts, transforms, gives life, brings to the light.

If the world is, as St Paul says, in the pangs of childbirth, how can I not regard the negative aspect which I now see as a hope of what will be?

Yes, we should affirm this clearly.

He has no faith in God –

who only believes in his own actions, who only believes in what can be seen;

he does not believe in the mystery, in God's potentiality, in God's invincible presence in history, in evolution.

In his heart, he does not believe in the parable of the prodigal son – for this is the parable of all mankind collectively, and hence of the victory of good over evil (cf. Lk 15).

––––––––––

And again:

Not hoping over the negative in man, only wanting to love the positive in him, sooner or later entails defeat.

I can say this for sure.

Let me give you an example:

Nowadays, an immense number of marriages break down a few years or even months after the wedding-day.

And I am not now talking about hasty marriages, cases of

hopeless incompatibility, marriages thoughtlessly entered
into, or non-Christian ones.

No, I mean proper marriages, grounded on Christian
faith, genuine Christian unions, true love, communion of
heart and soul, high minded motives etc.

Everything goes well for a little while and then you hear
people say, 'Yes, I did love her, we did love each
other. . . we were very happy. But now, I don't know. . . we
don't get on any more. We can't stick one another's company. It's like being married to a stranger, to someone I
don't seem to know. Perhaps we should be better off if we
parted. . .'

Hard words – but hiding a very simple phenomenon, especially today when psychology plays such an important
part in human relationships.

'I seem to be married to a stranger. . . someone I don't
know. . . I don't love him/her. . .'

To which I reply, 'You have only looked for the positive
in him/her. Now you've seen the negative, everything
comes unstuck.'

'You have gone about things the wrong way.'

Or rather, you ought to make a fresh start. . . if you want
to be saved. You ought to love his/her negative aspects, love
what is missing in the other.

You ought to help your partner to build him/herself, to
make him/herself. You ought to generate your partner in
true love.

Then you will love your marriage partner and love with
God's own love, and your love, because genuine, will then
be indestructible.

The time has come for you to rediscover your partner, to
bring your partner to birth from the poor creature's
negative aspects – that poverty, that wretchedness.

You will see that 'what is' has no connexion with what
will be, with what is not yet.

Try it. . .

God will help you, since he is the source.

You must encounter each other in reality – and this is not where you originally met, but much more true to life and much more interesting.

Remember that no one who cannot take this step will ever be able to love his brother for long.

Nothing is easier than to discover somebody's negative aspects.

But love, real love, begins from here and from these you have to reconquer the beloved.

Then your union will not be fragile and ephemeral but true and everlasting.

In another ten years, we must take a second honeymoon.

This is real love, now.

You end by loving as God loves.

And I have become aware of this because I love your poverty more than your beauty, your suffering more than your joy, your potentiality more than your actuality, your aspirations more than your ephemeral actions.

And so need to give myself

The difference between immature and mature love, between a baby's love and a mother's love, is that the former sucks and the latter is sucked; the former seeks, wants, exploits; the latter gives, endures, is emptied.

Taking is a sign of immature love; giving is love at its fullest.

The path from human selfishness, self-regarding, exploiting everything and everyone, to eventual self-giving is a long one, as long as history itself.

And often it doesn't make a pretty tale, since it results from efforts to get, rather than from successes in giving.

We are all involved in this, and few can boast of having given much.

Generally speaking, we are suffocating in selfishness and much of our unhappiness is due to our inability to give ourselves without reserve.

We find it hard to love because of sin, which is a very reversal of values, a basic disorder of the Kingdom within us.

We are creatures, yet think of ourselves as creators (pride).

We are brothers, yet want to be owners (avarice).

We are designed for freedom, yet are enslaved to our senses and to ourselves (lust).

No, loving isn't easy with a mind like ours, with a heart like ours, with sensuality like ours.

And so, we do not love and, not loving, feel we are in hell.

Hell is the lack of love.

Real love is rare.

Rarer than real faith.

It is man's maximum potential, here below.

The most difficult thing.

When man loves, he is like God but, just as it is hard to do what God does, so it is hard to love.

This is what happens.

The ray of real love, called charity, leaves God and reaches us.

Reaching us, it prompts us to make a gift of ourselves.

But it has to pass through the opaqueness of our body.

It comes out distorted.

Distorted by selfishness, avarice, pride.

It came into us with right intentions. . . coming out of us. . .

It isn't too much to say that out of a hundred acts defined as love proceeding from us, ninety-nine are polluted by selfishness, possessiveness or vanity.

What little manages to escape being distorted by these adverse forces, retains the character of real love, of self-giving.

But this is not an everyday event.

All the same, we must not be discouraged.

If I have taken the wrong road, I must turn back.

And in so doing, I shall realise something which is very important: everything has its uses, even sin.

Yes, even error can play its part in salvation.

God can even use sin to his glory.

If it were not so, we should all be lost.

I honestly believe that most people's salvation is effected by the stench of their sins and the bitterness of their innumerable defeats.

God's logic proceeds more obviously through the wreckage caused by our illogicality.

God affirms his existence by the very weight of our denials.

Heaven manifests itself by the noisesome darkness of our earthliness.

'*It has done me good to have to suffer*' (Ps 119:71): I can say after my every error, now become my ally against my pride.

'*No soundness in my flesh, I am worn out*' (Ps 38:7–8): I can realise in my revels; and my body, betrayed by me into sensuality, becomes my servant for penance and repentance.

'*O for the wings of a dove, far away would I fly to the wilds*' (Ps 55:6–7): I wish to cry each time I undergo the tyranny of idols.

And yet I must prepare to love.

I cannot do less, since this is the end to which I have been created.

'*Remember, O Israel: "You are to love your God with all your heart, with all your mind, with all your strength".*

'*This is the first life-giving commandment and the second is like it: "You are to love your neighbour as yourself."* '

(Mt 23:35–39)

Loving means identifying oneself with God.

Loving means entering the Kingdom.

The history of the world is the history of love.

The history of man is the history of love.

But for love like this to be achieved in us, to conquer us in its creative, very pure, transparent, free, divine vortex, it needs time to develop historically, patiently, freely.

From the violence of sex to the impetuosity of sentiment,

from the equilibrium of reason to the attraction of beauty,

from the demand made by liberty and freedom to the folly of the Cross, ever upwards, step by step,

love is refined, becomes transparent, participating more and more in the mode of being and loving of the One who created love and who is increate love, I mean, God.

God's mode of being as Love is the Holy Spirit, proceeding from Life which is the Father, and from the Son who is Light.

And this is so transparent as to be invisible to us.

And to make it visible, needed the Incarnation.

Hence the word became flesh and dwelt among us, and took our path beside us, and was called Jesus.

Jesus is God's love made man, hence visible to all men.

Jesus loves as God loves.

Jesus is the perfect mode of loving.

Jesus can teach us how to love.

Jesus is love incarnate.

Man who for way of loving had body, heart and spirit, now for way has God himself in Jesus.

Doing as Jesus did, he can achieve the highest degree of love.

Listening to the Spirit of Jesus dwelling within him, he can share in that same eternal life, which is knowledge and love of that same God shared by him and Jesus.

The perspective is completely altered, for the very root from which love springs has been changed.

Before, the root was below, now it is above.

Before, it was on earth, now in heaven.

Before, it was nature, now grace.

Before, it was self-interested, now free.

Before, it was time, now eternity.

Before, it was pleasure, now the Cross.

Before, it was self-seeking, now it seeks our brother.

Before, it was what pleases, now what displeases.

Before, it was the flesh, now the spirit.

Before, commotion, now peace.

Before, temporary gratification, now eternal joy.

Of course, things are not easy, and to understand their scope and difficulty, we have only to remember that Jesus himself had to die.

He did not talk just for the fun of talking: he actually died.

And he died voluntarily.

He died to alert us to the fact that our eternal salvation depends on whether we do or do not accept love's law: '*Away with you, accursed ones, to the eternal fire, for I was hungry and you never gave me food, I was thirsty and you never gave me anything to drink*' (Mt 25:41f).

He died to teach us the way: '*I am the light of the world; anyone who follows me will not be walking in the dark; he will have the light of life*' (Jn 8:12).

He died to demonstrate his love for us: '*A man can have no greater love than to lay down his life for his friends*' (Jn 15:13).

He died to teach us how to love: '*Love one another, just as I have loved you*' (Jn 13:34).

He died for love.

Even if I am wicked and selfish,
even if I am weak and ineffectual,
that same demand is always in me: to die for love.

I hope to manage this – at least a few seconds before my physical death. Better still, if I could die a violent death for my God.

I continually ask this of the Lord, especially during the Eucharist, that is to say, when I communicate with the death and resurrection of Christ.

I know that dying of love is paradise.

I know that it is the Father's will.

I know that it is my eternal joy.

And hence it is, I set out on this road forthwith, to waste no time.

The road is Jesus's road.

It is an almost perpendicular descent, the exact opposite of the path that men recommend me to take.

When Jesus seeks man, he descends.

Descends in the Incarnation and becomes a slave.

Descends in the Lord's Supper and becomes bread.

Descends among men and becomes the lowest.

The place chosen by Jesus is the lowest one: Bethlehem, Nazareth, Calvary.

He is not born mighty, he sees the light of day in a stable.

He doesn't belong to an influential family, he works for a living; he doesn't try to conquer, he loses his life on the cross.

This is how love behaves, only satisfied by touching rock-bottom: the lowest place.

Father de Foucauld used to say of Jesus, '*He chose so much the lowest place that no one can ever deprive him of it.*' All the same, we can try to get near him.

Between the well-off and the poor, Jesus chooses the poor.

Between the healthy and the sick, Jesus chooses the sick.

Between the well-fed and the starving, Jesus chooses the starving.

Make no mistake about it.

And this is why the Gospel choice leaves us no choice but to be on the right side: the side of those who are the lowest, who suffer most, who are most cut off from society, who have greatest need of someone.

Much suffering in the Church today is due to our awareness of not always being on the right side.

The sight of the bishop living in a palace.

The awareness that our congregation has more money than novices.

The realisation that most Christians live in the world's wealthier countries.

This makes us all feel uneasy.

And strange it is that, no sooner has some young man pointed this out and protested, then instead of telling him that he is perfectly right to be angry about it, the congregation locks up its account-books, while 'right-thinking Christians' cling to the notion that charity needs money and that without money nothing can be done.

But these days, it is harder to ignore the protest in the Gospel itself.

The lowest place is the lowest place, and he who means to follow Christ must make the same choice of poverty as he did, and no longer take cover behind the usual excuse of 'the dignity of the Church'.

The dignity of power, of impressive ceremonies, may have served for a Church still in its childhood – the Church of the Middle Ages – but becomes counter-productive in a mature Church such as ours, born of the tremendous suffering and lucidity of the contemporary world and the Council.

The prayer of abandonment which I recite each evening with my brothers in faith, says at this point:

'*I need to give myself*'.

It isn't easy to say this truthfully and spiritually.

All our weakness comes between.

And just because we do feel weak, we gather in groups, we become the Church.

And to help each other, we become a congregation.

I became a Little Brother, so as not to be alone.

And I assure you that I have not felt alone in my attitude of wanting to give myself to the poorest and the lowliest.

To surrender myself into your hands without reserve

I have surrendered myself into man's hands by taking his part.

I have surrendered myself into the hands of the poor by taking the lowest place.

Is there anything more I can do?

Yes, there is something more.

The hands of man, the hands of the poor, still imply a reservation.

But there is a *'without reserve'*, a loving without reservation.

It is consent on man's part to hurling himself into the dark abyss, into the opaqueness of the creation.

It is the consent on Christ's part – the son – to being forsaken by the Father.

The tragic cry we hear in our own day is the very cry of Christ crucified.

'My God, my God, why have you forsaken me?' (Mt 27:46).

No amount of reasoning can explain this. It is useless to try and understand it.

It is useless to approach Job with our theological handbooks in the hopes of discovering the reasons for and explanation of his desperate suffering.

For Job himself will answer:

'Perish the day on which I was born, and the night when it was said, "A man has been conceived"! May that day be darkness, may God not remember it on high, may no light shine on it! May murk and deep shadow claim it, clouds hang over it, eclipse swoop down on it!'

(Jb 3)

There is nothing amusing about man's sufferings, the agony of his sleepless nights, his flesh tormented by the fires of pain, the terror of his darkened faith.

How can we not take the part of someone so sorely tried, without trying – like the right-minded – to defend God, to justify his reasons for inflicting suffering on mankind?

For He it is who strikes, and Job knows this.

On the face of things, the Sabaeans are responsible for having rustled his oxen.

And the lightning, for having burnt his flocks to death.

And the Chaldaeans, for putting his servants to the sword and making off with his camels.

But Job only sees the hand of God.

God it is who gives and takes away, God it is who strikes.

'Naked I emerged from my mother's womb, naked I shall return.
Yahweh gave, Yahweh has taken away. Blessed be the name of
Yahweh!'

(Jb 1:21)

But I do not want to try and justify God, and I cannot help taking man's part.

In any case, Job's dunghill is small in comparison with the dunghill of the world.

Man is born on a dunghill or, to be more horribly accurate, in a graveyard. Beneath him lie the bones of innumerable generations of animals and plants.

You might say that his body is composed of the detritus of death, battening on living things for thousands of centuries before him.

The earth on which I am born, to my visionary eye appears a tormented sphere of clay kneaded by fire.

Geological eras follow one another, generating, transforming, designing, destroying incessantly, like successive impulses straining after something still to be done, a model not yet achieved, a face not yet completely formed.

I know what is to come, and faith is what tells me this — but what would he see who has no faith?

The fiery sphere is generating the son.

Following one another with inexhaustible impetus, the eras are forging his face.

And it is the face of Christ.

And it is the face of man, modelled on the face of Christ.

The whole creation is made to make us sons of God, and all the weariness, the torment, the temporariness, the suffering, is needed for the generative process to be achieved.

But at what a cost!

And beyond the cost, what hope must animate him who is on the inside of such toil, who cannot see it from outside, who is trapped in thousands on thousands of continuous, inky contradictions!

Can you wonder that the suffering forces shrieks from man and makes the very fibres of his being tremble?

Can you wonder that he gazes wildly into the darkness, shouting, '*My God, my God, where are you? Why don't you answer from your sealed heavens?*'

Man is spirit, in a vessel of clay: how can he not be aware of his weakness?

Man is a saint in a '*body of death*': how can he not be in pain?

Man is a log of wood to be transformed into fire: how can he not be in torment?

As I said, I have no desire to justify God for all the muddle which I observe in the creation and for all the contradictions to which he submits me, but I also know that God has not sought and does not seek any justification.

He says nothing.

How terrible, God's silence in man's darkness!

This is perhaps the worst suffering of all.

Certainly, it is the most heroic of ordeals.

It is the '*without reserve*' which sooner or later he demands of us.

It is the darkness.

It is darkness falling on man's body and spirit, tearing at him, torturing him.

Job, in his agony, says to God:

> '*He has made me his target;*
> *he shoots his arrows at me,*
> *pitilessly piercing my sides,*
> *shedding my gall on the ground.*
> *Opening wound after wound,*
> *he attacks me like a warrior.*
> *I have sewn sacking over my skin*
> *and flung my forehead in the dust.*
> *My face is reddened with weeping*
> *and shadow hangs on my eyelids.*

(Jb 16:12–16)

And what do the dying say to Him?

People locked up in madhouses, human vegetables in chronic wards, the skeletal bodies of the aged, the misshapen, the children with Down's syndrome, the dwellers on the fringes of society, the cripples and the blind walking the streets of the world?

What do those people say to him who seek without finding, who have no hope, who have no faith, who couple alive and yet are dead?

I don't know.

Everyone tries to give an answer, but God for his part does not put the question.

He says nothing.

And he says nothing, even when it is his beloved, his only Son Jesus who is concerned.

'*My God, my God, why have you forsaken me?*' – and his cry is the concentrated cry of all mankind.

God says nothing.

And the sphere of clay goes on being kneaded by the fiery
hands,
the living die,
the young grow old,
sunset goes on following sunrise,
heaven goes on reflecting earth
and the stars go on looking down on us as though nothing
were happening.
Nothing stirs.
Far away in the silence, the agonised cry of Jesus echoes
on:
'My God, my God, why have you forsaken me?'

I have already told you. – Don't try to understand, you
won't succeed.
Don't try to see; you won't see.
Try to love.
In love and only in love can we be near Jesus Forsaken
and with him be near all the world's forsaken.
But, please, not just to shed a sympathetic tear!
At sight of such a mystery, tears are not enough; the
Spirit must be there to tell and instruct me on the wherefore
of the price, to help me understand what is hidden under
man's crust of fiery clay.
Speak, O Spirit of God, reply to Jeremiah as he tells you
his story – a story much the same as any of ours.

'God. . . God. . .
has flung me to the ground,
has made a yoke for me
and has clamped my head in a vice.
God. . . God. . .
bending his bow
has taken aim at me
as target
for his arrows.

God... God...
has broken my teeth
on gravel,
and if I cry and groan,
he stifles, stifles
my prayer.
See what gall and wormwood
have reduced me to
in this my fleeting life...
What will become of me
if hope should fail,
that hope
which comes from Yahweh?
Sit silent and alone
since Yahweh imposes this.
Put your lips to the dust —
perhaps there is still hope.
Offer your cheek
to the striker.
For Yahweh does not cast us off
for ever and ever.
Even if he punishes,
he has mercy afterwards.

What will become of me
if hope should fail,
that hope
which comes from Yahweh?'

(cf Lm 3)

Here you see the price exacted for the masterpiece being prepared for mankind by God: hope, which comes from the Lord. And the Lord stays silent because that hope is growing and developing.

The ability to hope is the greatest gift that God could make to man.

When man is endowed with hope, he overcomes the obstacles in which he is ensnared.

When man hopes, he dies already seeing his body in the resurrection light.

When man hopes, he overcomes fear, understands the purpose of ordeal, puts his trust in God, believes in things which are impossible, feels God's presence in his darkness, begin to pray.

Abraham's hope is one of the wonders of mankind, and the hope of the martyrs is the radiance of the Church.

Hope is born when man experiences the abyss of his helplessness, as Israel did in Babylon, as Jeremiah when lowered into the prison cistern, as Jesus on the Cross.

And now I approach Jesus Forsaken with greater understanding. In him, I see all the world's sufferings concentrated, the redemptive fire of mankind in evolution, the key to love's greatest secret.

In him, I have the answer to things which have no answer. In him, the soothing away of all my questions, the receptacle of all my brothers' sufferings, the most sublime exemplar of Yahweh's poor man, the heroic mission of the true remnant of Israel, man made truly son of the Most High.

In this book I should like to have included, as bookmarker, a picture of the Holy Shroud, since that is the nearest in spirit to what I am seeking.

I believe, having studied the picture for many years, that it is a 'genuine photograph of Jesus'.

Ammoniac gasses, combining with the aloes and myrrh with which the body of Jesus had been treated on that Good Friday evening, produced a contact-print on the sheet in which he had been wrapped and laid in the tomb.

What remains is a negative, excluding all possibility of fraud.

As I said, I believe this to be a photograph of Jesus Crucified.

Though I would be prepared to say with Cardinal

Pellegrino, who introduced a television programme on the subject, 'If the photograph is not of Jesus, it is undeniably the photograph of a man who has suffered much, been crucified, been scourged and crowned with thorns.'

It comes to the same thing.

How wonderful to think that the photograph of Christ should be indistinguishable from that of the Man of Sorrows!

It is very dear to me.

This is why I keep the photograph on the table in my cell. Looking at it, I think of Jesus representing me in the Father's presence.

'*I surrender myself into your hands without reserve.*'

For I love you, Lord

My God, how much I love you.

And yet how much I wish I loved you more!

How often have I wept for sweetness when you have come near me, and how often have I felt you as though far away!

I can say that you are what I most desire, although I still desire too many other things besides you.

You are my all, and I am still far from being yours and from abandoning myself to you without reserve.

With you, I feel that I am Israel.

Israel's history has been my history from the days when Israel was called Jacob.

Like Jacob, I have lived in tents, and one night I too have seen the ladder reaching up, up into heaven with your angels coming down it (cf Gn 28:12).

Like Jacob, I have been at the Ford of Jabbok (cf. Gn 32:23) and, like him, wrestled with you throughout the night and experienced the impassible gulf separating man from God.

Having striven with you, I now have the three things, which you impressed on Jacob, impressed on my heart too:

1. *You have realised how weak you are*
2. *You will lean on God*
3. *You will conquer* (cf. Gn 32:23–33).

and hence I have taken that new name which you gave him that night he crossed the ford: Israel.

And in that name was my own destiny.

It was my personal destiny because it was the destiny of the New Israel: the Church.

I feel myself to be the Church, and in the Church I have relived the history of Israel, and the same so dramatic, so abysmal relationship of love: desert – exodus – promised land – temple – deportation – hope.

And always in the light of the three truths already stated:

1. You are now aware how weak you are.
2. Lean on God
3. You will conquer

And in respect of the first of these three truths, because it is so inherently part of you, you carry it in your flesh and spirit as second nature.

Sin's painful prodding is never far away.

'O Yahweh,
my sin has landed on my head, too heavy a burden for me; I have stinking, festering wounds, thanks to my folly' (Ps 38:4–5).

Weakness is the very heritage of man and goes on being that heritage even when man becomes the Church, even when he becomes the People of God.

What a lot of harm it did me, what a lot of my time it wasted: my childhood vision of the Church.

As a boy, I was received into a Church in which it was forbidden to tell the bitter truth. . . to tell it to the Church, because the Church was perfect.

In such an atmosphere, I got the impression that the *'immaculate and holy'* Church actually existed in the men who represented her.

How was the vision to be reconciled with everyday reality?

With the sins of shepherds *'who fed themselves and deserted the flock'*, with medieval popes, nepotists to the marrow, with despotic priests who looked on their parish as their private fief and the People of God as a 'vulgus indoctus' or as a purse to be exploited?

No, the face of the *'immaculate and holy'* Church is that of another Church – one that certainly exists, since Christ founded her and keeps her safe – existing in the heart, and in the gentleness and mercy of the Holy Spirit, who generates her and sustains her life.

This is the face of the Church as bride of God.

Of a God accustomed, as mothers are, ever to looking at the best side of their erring sons and to throwing a veil of love over their mischief – as Sarah did with Jacob – so that their father can go on cherishing the image of a beloved son.

No, the face of the immaculate and holy Church is that of a mysterious Church with a supernatural and divine personality, set by God's love in the heart of every one of his people, which people by virtue of this becomes *'a people of saints, of prophets, of priests'* (cf. 1 P 2:9).

But what I actually see is very different and I must not confuse the two, or otherwise that Church becomes a demon of pride.

And perhaps it is precisely so that we shouldn't become demons of pride that God leaves a crust of sin on my face, on the Church's face.

And this is why none of us, individually, can or should identify himself with the Church.

The Church is always beyond our poor human actuality and no one can represent her in her plenitude here below.

The Vatican would be wrong to say, 'I am the Church' for by so doing it would give me an inaccurate notion of her.

And I for my part, how can I identify myself with this *'holy city, the New Jerusalem, coming down as a bride adorned for her husband'* (Rv 21:2)?

Poor wretch that I am!

How sincerely I ask pardon of all who have got an ugly impression of God's Church from looking at me!

Fortunately my hope never falters, nor my leaning on you, my God, my essential need, my unquenchable thirst, my ever more lively and comforting experience,

'O Yahweh, my refuge, my eyrie,
my God in whom I put my trust'

(Ps 91:2)

'Yahweh is my shepherd,
what more can I want!
In green fields will he make me rest,
by quiet waters guide me,
there to refresh my soul'.

(Ps 23:1–3)

What however is more difficult to grasp is the third promise: *'You will conquer.'*
How does Israel conquer?
How does the Church conquer?
How do I conquer?
The answer to such questions has been as vexed as the history of Israel, as the history of the Church herself.
The Israelites originally supposed that the way for them to conquer was the same way as the world's, in which they were submerged: the conquest of earthly actuality, political domination of neighbouring peoples.
This was the way of force and strength, and Moses made the history of the People of God a history of conquest: the conquest and colonisation of the Land of Canaan; at the same time, he liberated the People of God from slavery.
The Church, the New Israel, followed the same path and, unintentionally perhaps, became the Mistress of nations.
Think of the prince-bishops, of the popes wielding sovereign power, of Christians who, 'taking the Cross', buckled on the sword!

Was that the way to conquer?

It was one way, certainly, but it's hard to say that it was the best, that it was the way hidden in God's will and revealed in the Gospel.

When I think about all that, I seem to be gazing into chaos, that very chaos preceding the creation and human history.

But over this chaos, I see the dove of the Spirit descending, who can impose order on things by his love.

And order is born in time and space,
is born as growth,
is born as becoming,
is born as 'sign'.
The earth is the sign of another earth,
home is the sign of another home,
human marriage is the sign of another marriage.

Even Israel is a sign.

Even the Church is a sign.

And for her to become a sign, she had to be made visible.

For her to understand freedom, she had to be set free.

For her to contemplate the Heavenly Jerusalem, the earthly Jerusalem had to be built.

But the sign once seen invites you to go beyond: the sacrament reminds you of Christ, the earth reminds you of heaven, human love invites you to think of God's love.

What then does the sign of the Promised Land say to me?

What does the sign of freedom say to me?

One thing only: that the Promised Land, the true one, is far beyond the Jordan,

and that being freed from slavery is something more fundamental than what occurred on the banks of the Nile.

The desire to turn back, to oppose the flow of history, far from being the will of God, is a return to chaos.

Israel, conquering the Promised Land by force of arms, as it has done, after two thousand years of stress, may

represent a military or political fact, but as a religious fact
is an absurdity and scandal.

As it would be equally absurd for the Church to renew its
demands for the temporal power of the pope and to re-
create the Papal States.

Go beyond – the sign tells me.

Do not look, O Israel, at that scrap of land called
Palestine, look at me, your God.

I am your Promised Land.

I am your Promised Land, even if you live in Moscow or
New York.

I am your Promised Land, even if you are not a kingdom,
even if you are the smallest and weakest of all the kingdoms
in the world.

Do not let yourself, O Christian, be dazzled by what is
temporal, look at what does not change, at my presence in
you and Christ's presence in the poor.

What maturity of vision!

What messianic times are ours!

It is as though we had outgrown the childhood of world
and Church alike!

You might say that we are now beginning to understand
the mystery of the 'signs', especially as concerns the Church
and the potentialities of her identifying herself with her present structure, weakened almost to vanishing point by the
power and fire of the Gospel.

––––––––––

My God, I love you!

As Israel loves you.

As the Church loves you.

And I thank you for having set me free from useless
things and letting me perceive your Divine Being more
clearly.

To Aaron you said,

'*You are to have no heritage in that land,*

no portion of it is to be yours,
I myself shall be your portion and your heritage'

(Nb 18:20)

Repeat this to me, my God, repeat this to the New Israel, the Church.

'*I myself am your heritage*'

Yes, O Lord, and I want no other. I desire you alone.

This is what the Church must say, '*I want you alone, my bridegroom, my light, my strength, my All*'.

The days of formality, of weighty trappings, of outward distractions, of useless plaster statues and childish processions, are over.

Yourself, be our reality.

Yourself, be our joy.

You without things interposed.

You without power politics.

Free as birds.

Walking the world's streets with the poor

with the hungry

with the suffering

with the persecuted.

Taking the true way to freedom with them.

With you, O Eucharist, celebrated in the intimacy of man's home, and sitting at your table where you make us partakers of your body and blood,

with you in our exile, which must last until you return,

with you, our heritage, our strength, our sweetness, our father.

And with boundless confidence

God has no difficulty in trusting man, but man finds it hard to trust God.

Hence, God's great patience towards us, and our inherent fear.

Man's real sin lies in not believing, in not hoping in, God.

Unbelief, scepticism, forms the basis of his relations with God.

If man trusted God, even if only as much as he trusts a friend on the town council or member of Parliament, he would never fear anyone again.

Instead!

God on the other hand has so much faith in man that he can always find a way-out for him, even in the most calamitous situations.

God's hope in man binds him not even to pass judgment on him, except at the end, the very end.

'*I have not come to judge the world but to save it*' (cf. Jn 3:17), Jesus was to say, he being God's mercy, God's hope, God's trust.

When Jeremiah ponders the history of Israel and cannot understand why the wheel should have taken so painful a turn, God leads him into a potter's shop.

'*Yes, as the clay is in the potter's hand, so are you in mine, House of Israel*' (Jr 18:6).

And when the pot cracks in the potter's hand or falls short of the original design, Jeremiah sees that the potter doesn't destroy the clay but remoulds it to another design.

God never abandons his clay.

All the time, he hopes to be able to make something out of that clay.

He himself made that clay at the Genesis of life: '*Then Yahweh God formed man from clods in the soil and into his nostrils blew the breath of life*' (Gn 2:7), producing a curious mixture of earth and spirit.

What troubles over that mixture!

What crackings – what botchings!

But God keeps remaking the mixture, he never gives up.

'*I tell you most solemnly, unless a man is born through water and the Spirit, he cannot enter the Kingdom of God*' (Jn 3:5), as though needing to be constantly regenerated.

Man – earth and spirit – may flee where he will, may blaspheme as he will, may hide where he will, but God's hope, God's trust, follows him wherever that is and awaits him.

And he knows exactly what to do, since he is Love.

As we have already said, man finds it hard to trust in God.

And he has to learn: his life depends on it.

Trusting in God means peace, joy, serenity, security, strength.

Not trusting means loneliness, sadness, fear.

As unbelief is overcome by faith, so trust is nourished by hope.

The theological virtues given us by God are the appropriate means by which we attain the states of believing, hoping and loving.

We are like the crew of a spaceship, launching out of Earth's orbit to where disbelief is overcome, scepticism fades away and real love, charity, conquers us for good.

If launch-off is difficult, even if the flight is tough, the ex-

perience gained by each victory of faith brings us deep joy.
After each effort of believing, hoping and loving, we are left
with a sense of security and courage.

And this is when, like Moses escaping alive from the Red
Sea, I want to sing:

> *'Yah is my strength, my song,*
> *to him I owe my salvation.'*   (Ex 15:2)

Like David, I express my confidence:

> *'The Lord is my shepherd,*
> *what more can I want?'*   (Ps 23:1)

Like Jonah, my victorious prayer:

> *'In my distress,*
> *I cried to Yahweh*
> *and he answered me.'*   (Jon 2:3)

And like Mary, my joy:

> *'Great is the Lord, my soul proclaims,*
> *with all my heart I exult in God my Saviour.'*
>   (Lk 1:46)

Anything seems easy to me, then, once having decided to
go with God to the world's end.
Like Peter, I say to Jesus:

> *'With you, Lord, I am ready to go to prison and death'.*
>   (Lk 22:33)

And, with Paul, I repeat in the Spirit:

> *'Who can separate us from the love of God?'*
>   (Rm 8:35)

If only I could stay constant to these sentiments!

If I could never change again, if I could be steadfast in this grace!

But I can't.

In an hour's time, I shan't be like this anymore.

Perhaps in an hour's time, I shall have become a prey to aridity, reestablishing its empire over my heart, or to darkness, into which I shall relapse.

Nothing is stable here below, nothing definitely saved.

This is an exodus.

But, as in the Exodus, there are footmarks marking out the road.

The footprints of past experience.

A memory carved like an inscription on the rocks along my way.

Remember, O Israel (Exodus).

Yes, I remember. . . I remember the Red Sea, I remember the Waters of Meribah, I remember the manna.

The memory reminds me to have confidence.

The difficulty we have in trusting God is the same difficulty we have in trusting man, our brother-man.

We never succeed in overcoming this, and our scepticism as regards man is the source of our aridity and joylessness.

We have no faith in that blessed mixture of earth and spirit standing before us.

We only see its defects.

We do not believe that a well-made and even useful vessel can come out of this clay.

And the root of this too is lack of faith in the hands of the craftsman, who is God and, let us never forget, the God of the Impossible.

Our God – and this is why he is so weak – is the God of the Possible; we still, alas, do not know the God of the Impossible.

Our God is still conceived in the measure of man, not in

the measure of a Creator able to give us the marvels of successive dawns and the earthquake of the resurrection.

Hence, it is even harder for us to trust in our brothers.

'*Can anything good come out of Nazareth?*' (Jn 1:46), Nathaniel was to say to the man who told him about the Nazarene.

We are always convinced that from certain places, from certain natures, from certain types, from certain situations, no good can come.

And so we are mistrustful.

And we are afraid of anything new, especially if we are decent, well-organised, learned, and above all if we are occupying a position of authority.

In all my experience, for instance, I have never seen people who were more reluctant to accept anything new than certain types of parents and churchmen. The fact is that so-called 'sinners' more easily accept change in a spirit of faith than so-called 'good people'. And this is so much the case that I now believe that most 'confrontation' is provoked – certainly unintentionally and possibly even unwittingly – by the rigidity and security of the latter, and most especially by their unwillingness to put any confidence in the opinions of people younger than or subordinate to themselves.

I think St Paul's recommendations to the Colossians (3:21) can rarely have been more apposite than in our own times of transition and change: 'Fathers, do not antagonise your children, lest they become discouraged' – for now is a time when the young – and not only the young – are discouraged.

There is indeed – make no doubt about it – a crisis of authority!

And it won't be easy to re-knit the old web of trust, which used to hold society and the Church herself together.

We shall have to try and have more imagination and courage, instead of preaching so many sermons about obedience. If, for instance, it is realised that expenditure on building an enormous church is going to cause scandal to the young, the scheme should be abandoned until times seem more propitious. And if the mature People of God feel the need to develop their independence of mind in the political sphere, and to exercise greater freedom in civil matters, it would be wiser to confine ourselves to advising and not take one side rather than another.

It is not always possible, furthermore, to make religious law coincide with the laws of the State; and Christian respect and tolerance for sinners is not to be shrugged off by anyone claiming to follow Jesus, who even allowed himself to be put to death by the wicked.

How hard it is to have faith in my brother-man!

What inner gymnastics I have to perform to convince myself that from him, still perhaps a capitalist like Zacchaeus, or from her, still a prostitute like Mary Magdalen, tomorrow's saint can be born.

It is certainly a sign of age, if I do not have faith in tomorrow's young.

It would also be a sign of the Church's age, were she not to hope that salvation is at work in our generation too and that the Spirit has already implanted similar dispositions, far away from us, at the remotest limits of the earth, in the poorest man, '*the little remnant of Israel*', able to welcome the coming of the Eternal Messiah, the Christ of God, Jesus Risen from the dead.

Yes, I should have faith in man, since having faith in him proves that I have confidence in God.

And having faith in Moslems proves that I believe that their history has meaning, since also made by God and based like ours on Abraham.

Having full faith in people far away, I find the strength to feel that they already belong to the one great human family redeemed by Jesus.

Having faith in people who do not think as I do, I find a

file for sharpening my own thought and for re-inforcing myself in the truth.

And finally, having faith in today's atheists, I find in them the caustic soda for scrubbing the mythological paraphernalia and superstitious accretions off my own religious edifices, reducing my hope to the pure and simple glad news of the Gospel.

Trusting in man and in his ability to be converted, witnesses in daily life to my confidence in God.

For you are my Father

Under the Old Covenant, God offered mankind a relationship with the invisible, which was typified by marriage.

Yahweh was Israel's husband, and the People of God prided themselves on their marital intimacy with him, the Song of Songs being the finest expression of this allegory.

In the New Covenant, the offer was a different one: the fatherhood of God.

And Jesus speaking of God no longer uses the imagery of husband but calls him Father.

When you pray, pray like this, 'Our Father'.

Christ is the Son.

God is the Father.

And, as Jesus was a son, so mankind is offered the opportunity of becoming sons.

'But to those who accept him, he gives the power of becoming sons of God. For these are born, not of the urge of the flesh or will of man, but of God' (Jn 1:12–13).

I have to admit that my original attachment to the Yahweh-Israel relationship, which I used to think of as a marriage between God and me, made me slow to grasp the value of the new relationship propounded by Jesus in the Gospel.

I did not realise its depth and breadth.

It was hidden from me by my all-preoccupying theocentricity.

Preoccupied with my search for the vision of God, I

forgot about my brother standing beside me; to bother about him struck me as unimportant.

Then there came a flash – I remember the day – and for the first time I said the Lord's Prayer in a completely different way.

In expounding the theme of God's fatherhood to me, Jesus did not alter Israel's relationship to him – for as an image of intensity, the one of marriage was perfectly adequate – but he changed the relationship between me and my brothers.

If God was a father, he was not the father of a tiny family with circumscribed human preoccupations!

If God was a Father, that meant that his sons were really my brothers, not 'in flesh and blood' but in the new divine reality propounded to me by God himself.

Henceforth, these my brothers were of nature divine, and for me to take no interest in them, to offend them, not to serve them, involved the same degree of wickedness as not to take an interest in, to offend, not to serve, the Father.

For the first time, I really understood the essential connection between the first and second commandments.

I had heard it asserted often enough; but now, I actually felt it.

This was something quite different.

———

By telling me that God is our father, Jesus puts the divinity of the whole human family on a sure footing, carrying the relationship between man and man to its extreme logical conclusion.

This is the light in which I understand the violent finality of his words:

'Away with you, accursed ones,
to the eternal fire,
for I was hungry
and you never gave me food. . .'

(Mt 25:41f)

Not to feed my brother, to refuse him food, is like refusing food to God himself as he goes past me holding out his hand.

The sin against man is the same sin against God.

Man and God belong to the same family.

Which happens to be my family too.

There is no way of getting away from this: my brother is really and truly my brother.

Mankind now looks completely different to me. Now I say: I desire the human family to be at one.

I cannot hold on to my money if my brother asks me for it.

If I have two coats, I have to give one of them to the man who hasn't got one.

Universal equality is the divine law.

Universal brotherhood – constant tension.

But there is more to it than this.

My brother is the Church with me, since the Church is the symbol of the universal heavenly reunion to which we are called as sons of God, and towards which we journey.

Everything is seen in a new light.

My brother is the sacrament of the Church, the visible sign of my love.

I must share the bread of Earth and bread of Heaven with him.

With him, I share prayer and work, human solidarity, charity divine, those goods visible and those invisible.

The Church becomes the most wonderful of reunions, the most perfect of communities.

The place of God and of men.

The presence of Christ.

The love-feast.

The symbol of the heavenly banquet.

Christianity first springs into existence as Church – community – reunion.

The first Christians formed themselves into communities: the community of Jerusalem, of Antioch, of Ephesus, of Alexandria, of Thessalonica.

And these communities, as the Acts of the Apostles tell us, had four unmistakeable characteristics.

1. *They persevered in listening to the Apostles' teaching.*
2. *They were faithful to prayer.*
3. *They broke bread.*
4. *They owned everything in common, so that... no one went in need* (Ac 2:42–44).

What a magnificent idea!

Why not renew such hope in our own day?

Is it so impossible?

Wouldn't this be the way to escape from a life without direction, from a suffocating routine, from structures now senescent?

To live as a true Church.

To build a community on the same lines as the one described by St Luke, from the bishop down to the lowliest peasant in the remotest village.

No one should not be part of a community.

Everyone should be involved in building it.

See the bishop leaving his room at dawn and coming downstairs to pray.

He should not be alone in his chapel with his household. Round him should be his clergy – his community – as they were for Augustine at Hippo.

In the midst of this genuine community is where he ought to pray. Together, they should calmly and unhurriedly break the word of God as daily food and inspiration of their lives.

Then let us take an ordinary parish. In it there are one or

two religious communities, possibly very small ones barely capable of independent existence, groups of activists at the outset of their spiritual careers.

Why for instance not start the day by saying the Daily Office together?

Why this ridiculous insistence on everyone saying the Office on his or her own?

Wouldn't it be better for all to meet and spend an hour in genuine prayer, entrusting the expounding of the Word to someone competent and trying to create as thoroughly cordial a community as possible?

I think the time has come to think about this.

All convinced Christians should feel that they belong to a true community of prayer.

If the parish is alive, the community is there already; if dead or on its last legs, the thing to do would be to make a fresh start, with like-minded people forming a community based on friendship and fellow-feeling, and so up, to a pooling of resources and the breaking of bread together.

And here I want to say a few pointed words.

We must get rid of our fears.

Certain organisations believe themselves to be the unique repositories of newness.

If a community has not been born in their house, they do all they can not to recognise it.

They do the very opposite of what the Apostles did.

When the Apostles heard that there was a group of pagans who used to meet in Christ, they did not take offence, they did not impose a boycott, they sent Barnabas.

And Barnabas, '*on arrival, saw that God had bestowed grace – and was delighted*' (Ac 11:22).

Is it right to panic every time something new comes to birth in a parish?

Are we to believe that the Spirit rests uniquely on the man officially in charge?

And an equally sharp word must be said in the other direction: to those group-Churches which spring up without any contact with parish priest or bishop – as though this were almost a matter of principle.

It is all too easy to lose sight of one of the fundamental aspects of the Church, and indeed the one which the Acts of the Apostles lists as the first: '*They persevered in listening to the Apostles' teaching.*'

And this is a serious matter, certainly not in accord with the Spirit of Christ.

For, if we want the bishops to be ever more trusting and open to what is new, '*lest the Spirit be quenched*' now blowing consistently everywhere, we must encourage the various groups spontaneously springing up, to have faith in the bishops and involve them too in the great work of rebirth and communion as the post-Conciliar Church emerges from the pre-Conciliar one.

And this, not for the sake of obtaining the customary approbations or of being paid unctuous compliments, but of faithfully doing what Christ wishes us to do.

Without the bishop there is no Church, and we are certainly not doing God's will by unduly prolonging abnormal situations.

Cardinal Pellegrino has put it nicely: '*We are travelling together*', and this approach seems to me a perfect modern commentary on what the Fathers used to say and what St Augustine said so well: '*With you I am a Christian, and for you I am a bishop.*'

Making a community.

Belonging to a living community of love, prayer, Eucharist, service.

And above all, a community which is a Church.

When can we say that a group of men and women, young people and old, becomes a Church?

What is the difference between a group-Church and any other kind of group meeting for spiritual, cultural, political or recreational purposes?

The answer is simple.

The group becomes a Church when governed by the Word, like that first historic Christian community.

The Word of God, proclaimed in the community, summons the Spirit.

And the Spirit of the Lord makes the Church.

And in the Church we find the necessary aids for advancing in love.

In the Church we find unity.

We find the Eucharist.

In this, we nourish our faith, we live in hope and make our love ever truer.

It is difficult to live without the Church.

If you ask yourselves sincerely why Christians find life so hard today, you will have to agree that most of the difficulties arise from the isolation in which so many of them live.

They have no Church, or if they have, it is a parish stricken with hardening of the arteries and kept going to boost illusory statistics.

Many young people find no living entity in parish-life to be a Church for them.

Similarly, in religious communities, many individuals live lives of agonising isolation, for lack of unity, prayer and love.

There are convents, no longer communities of prayer.

There are monasteries where people pray, but no longer love one another.

There are families, where there is no communication.

How deadly a state of affairs this is for the Universal Church!

Priests who have no friends and who pray alone!

Bishops in their domestic chapels, saying vespers by themselves!

The death-note of the Christian community is this: celebrating the liturgy without a community, as a private act.

It is unimaginable.

It is like making a habit of always having supper alone.

It is a serious symptom of old age and of inability to grasp what is happening. . . or of egocentricity.

And to sum up the subject of the Church as community, let me make one point more.

It is no good sheltering in the old refrain: 'It's not my concern . . . I can't do anything about it . . . it's the priest's concern, the bishop's concern, my mother's concern.'

I think, it's everybody's concern.

The first symptom of conversion by which we prove that we have grasped what the Church actually is, is when we stop thinking about the Church as only being the Vatican or the diocese, and think of it as being each one of us.

We are the Church!

Each of us is the Church!

What power would be generated, were all Christians to keep saying, '*I am the Church*' and each to contribute something to the activities of the bishop, by saying, 'It concerns me.'

Now I am making a start.

Now I am trying to make a community.

I don't want to be on my own any more.

I want to have companions on my journey.

To live my life with them.

Even if there are only a few of us, I want to make a start.

We shall pray at home.

We shall read the Bible together.

We shall make the Eucharist what the first Christians made it.

We shall help each other.

We shall pool as much of our property as we can.

We shall live by the Gospel.

And I think that the acutely worrying problem of priestly vocations would soon be solved in a community of this sort.

A community of prayer.

A community-Church in which the faith is sincerely lived, automatically becomes a very seminary. Where the Word is proclaimed, the Spirit comes, and the task of the Spirit is to make a Church and distribute its graces within it.

I am absolutely convinced that the grace of the priesthood will manifest itself forthwith in any such community of mature faith and prayer – far sooner indeed than in those wan and anaemic colleges kept open merely for fear that vocations may dry up.

Communities born alive and fecund in our own day, such as the Taizé Community, the Bose Community, the Cursillos de Cristiandad, adult catachetic and refresher courses, the Charismatic groups, the Pro Civitate Christiana, the various Brotherhoods inspired by Father de Foucauld, and so on, have no problems as regards vocations. They have as many priests as they want and doubtless some to spare.

So why be afraid?

God is God and will not let his Church want for the necessary shepherds.

CONCLUSION

And now my task is almost done.

I wanted to write this book as a kind of testament.

I am now near the winning-post and my course is almost run.

Talking about my Father has been sweet and easy for me.

The extraordinary fact of the fatherhood of God and, even more, our promotion to being his sons has fascinated me and comforted me.

In it, I have found the explanation for what I have experienced in prayer as communication, as contemplation: genuine gestation in the womb of God.

There are no limits to his greatness and no words to express his dignity.

If I pray, I know now that I can do this because I am a son.

If I were not a son, I should not be able to pray, because I should not be able to communicate with him.

This is the secret which I want to share with my friends, so that they will not become discouraged when the heavens seem closed and the darkness too dense.

So that they may know that this is the darkness of childbirth and that he who is generating us is silent for choice, so that hope may be born in all its glory.

Ours is the task of being faithful and loyal, especially when prayer is hard and painful.

And I should like us to achieve solidarity as a Church.

In the Church which we love so much, though aware of all her faults and weaknesses.

What should we do without her?

The mystery of the Church is the mystery of our own grandeur and sin: of holiness and betrayal.

Never as today have I felt her so alive, so true, and never as today have I been more aware of her rigidity.

But no one in the world has the power to separate me from her, just as no one in the world has the power to separate me from Christ.

And in this spirit I should like to ask pardon of those of my brothers whom I may have unintentionally scandalised in these hard and troublous times.

It isn't easy to live according to the Gospel, to follow its teachings and put them into practice.

It isn't easy to exercise responsibility, torn by the intransigence of one's own conscience on the one hand, and consideration for other people, particularly those farthest away.

And sometimes, mutual understanding, patient trust and infinite tolerance are absolutely essential.

Jesus commands us not to judge, and never has that command seemed so essential for the healthy survival of the Church.

With the Council, a more mature Church was born than the Church of our childhood.

A Church in which plurality is accepted, where there is respect for everyone, even for those who do not believe.

A Church in which charity for and solidarity with our brothers are more important than details of ritual and legal niceties.

A Church to be the Gospel.

A Church to be hope.

A Church to be love.

Also from Orbis . . .

SILENT PILGRIMAGE TO GOD
The Spirituality of Charles de Foucauld

By a Little Brother

'This will introduce Charles de Foucauld to many who have not met him before, and act as a guide to the essentials of his faith for many who have already made some contact. . .

'The greater part is his own letters and diaries, prayers and meditations. . .

'This book, with its burning words and piercing message, c

c